MILTON

SUPER CHAMPION

ACKNOWLEDGMENTS

MY THANKS GO TO EVERYONE WHO HAS HELPED ME IN THE
RESEARCH OF THIS BOOK, PARTICULARLY JOHN WHITAKER, TOM
AND DOREEN BRADLEY, WHO GAVE SO GENEROUSLY OF THEIR
TIME, AND BILL BROWN, MARTIN DRISCOLL, STEVE HADLEY AND
RON LONGFORD, WHO PASSED ON THEIR PERSONAL
RECOLLECTIONS OF THE EARLY LIFE OF THIS GREAT HORSE. I
HAVE ALSO RECEIVED INVALUABLE ASSISTANCE FROM JOHN
HARDING-ROLLS, MY COLLEAGUE GILLIAN NEWSUM AND FROM
NAOMI TAILBY AND ANNETTE BATCHELOR AT THE BSJA. MY
GRATITUDE, TOO, TO MANDY AND TONY REEMAN-CLARK,
GENEROUS KEEPERS OF THE FAX, AND AS ALWAYS TO HE WHO
OWNS THE COMPUTER.

PHOTO CREDITS

THE AUTHOR AND PUBLISHERS WOULD LIKE TO THANK THE
FOLLOWING PHOTOGRAPHERS WHO HAVE CONTRIBUTED TO
THIS BOOK:
ELIZABETH FURTH FOR THE PHOTOGRAPHS ON PAGES 6, 34, 44,
46, 68, 70, 74, 108, 126, 137 (LOWER), 150, 153
KIT HOUGHTON FOR THE PHOTOGRAPHS ON PAGES 8, 28, 98, 122
JAN GYLLENSTEN FOR THE PHOTOGRAPHS ON PAGES 37, 38–39,
41, 61, 85, 96 (RIGHT), 102, 128, 131, 132, 140
BOB LANGRISH FOR THE PHOTOGRAPHS ON PAGES 29, 31, 32–
33, 62, 64, 90, 91, 97, 113, 124 (LEFT), 137 (UPPER), 147
XAVIER LIBRECHT FOR THE PHOTOGRAPHS ON THE TITLE PAGE
AND PAGES 15, 51, 54–55, 59, 79, 93, 118–119, 121, 124 (RIGHT), 125
MAIL NEWSPAPERS FOR THE PHOTOGRAPH ON PAGE 11
EXPRESS NEWSPAPERS FOR THE PHOTOGRAPH ON PAGE 19
HORST RUDEL FOR THE PHOTOGRAPH ON PAGE 96 (LEFT)
JACKET PHOTOS
FRONT: JOHN WHITAKER AND MILTON WARM-UP AT HICKSTEAD
BACK: TOM AND DOREEN BRADLEY, PROUD OWNERS OF MILTON
BOTH PHOTOGRAPHS ARE BY ELIZABETH FURTH.

DESIGN: DESIGN/SECTION, FROME
TYPESETTING: SELWOOD SYSTEMS,
MIDSOMER NORTON
REPRODUCTION BY COLORCRAFT, HONG KONG
PRINTED AND BOUND BY BUTLER AND TANNER, FROME, ENGLAND

MILTON

SUPER CHAMPION

JUDITH
DRAPER

SBL

THIS EDITION FIRST PUBLISHED 1992 BY
SPRINGFIELD BOOKS LIMITED, NORMAN ROAD,
DENBY DALE, HUDDERSFIELD HD8 8TH, WEST
YORKSHIRE, ENGLAND

BRITISH LIBRARY CATALOGUING IN PUBLICATION
DATA

DRAPER, JUDITH
MILTON: SUPER CHAMPION
I TITLE
798.2092

ISBN 1 85688 029 X

CONTENTS

DORTMUND 1990: JOHN AND MILTON BRING THE WORLD CUP BACK TO EUROPE FOR THE FIRST TIME SINCE 1979

INTRODUCTION

'To be second to Milton is like being the winner.' Those words, spoken by legendary Brazilian rider Nelson Pessoa, eloquently sum up the esteem in which the world's leading riders hold one of the greatest horses ever to look through a bridle. Such is their admiration that Pessoa – hoping to crown his long and tremendously successful career with one more glorious victory – could, only minutes after seeing the 1991 World Cup slip from his grasp, beam good humouredly at the press and shrug off their proffered condolences with genuine admiration for his conqueror.

Never in the history of show jumping, or of any equestrian sport with the sole exception of racing, has one horse earned such unreserved plaudits from his adversaries or so totally beguiled the public. European gold medallist, twice World Cup holder, winner of virtually every important Grand Prix, one of the most consistent Nations Cup horses ever and the first show jumper to earn one million pounds in prize-money, Milton has without doubt become a legend in his lifetime.

Unbeatable? No. Consistently outstanding, yes. And as if sheer athletic brilliance were not enough, Milton has been blessed with that elusive, impossible-to-define something extra – charisma, star quality, call it what you will – that makes people catch their breath when he steps into the arena. If he were a human being, he would be in the Olivier, Fonteyn, Pavarotti league. Presence, panache, personality, he has it all. And more, for when they were handing out good looks, Milton must have been at the top of the list. Born dark grey, he has with age turned whiter and whiter until, in his teens, he resembles an exquisite piece of fine china. With his huge dark eyes, handsome head and unique floating style of jumping, he has bewitched crowds not just in Britain but throughout Europe and on the other side of the Atlantic.

In addition, Milton is one of those true equine stars who seems to know exactly how good he is. Far from being daunted by the adulation that is heaped upon him, he thrives upon it, growing in stature when he enters an arena to thunderous applause; turning his head, ears pricked, to eye the audience with interest; smiling for photographers during awards ceremonies while other horses look bored; playing to his public and accepting their ovations with quiet dignity. Like a prima ballerina taking a curtain call, he has been bombarded with bunches of flowers; he has been endlessly photographed, painted and sculpted; stroked, patted and even, once, prevailed upon to part with a few hairs of his tail. (These, suitably mounted and framed, became a much treasured possession not of a female teenage fan, but of an adult, male member of the organising committee of a major international show who was thrilled to bits.)

He is, in short, the complete performer. He has given his owners, Doreen and Tom Bradley, a tremendous fillip in their retirement years, easing the pain of their daughter Caroline's early death and providing a living testimony to her skill as a producer of competition horses.

To be second to Milton is, indeed, like being the winner.

MILTON'S PEDIGREE

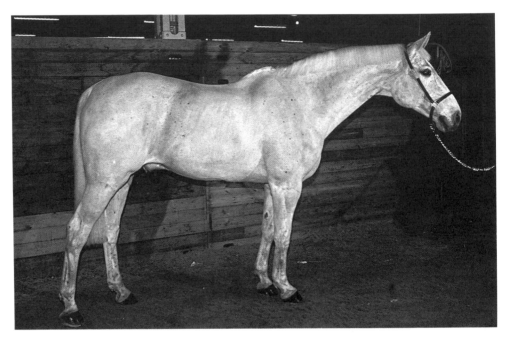

MILTON	MARIUS	MARCO POLO	POET (XX)	JANITOR
				PRISKA
			MIRAKEL (TRAK)	ALTAN
				MIRA
		OMINKA	SINAEDA	CAMILLUS
				MORGENSTER (HOLST)
			RAMINKA	FEINER KERL (OLD)
				FREIMINKA (OLD)
	ASTON ANSWER (EPAULETTA)	ANY QUESTIONS	QUESTIONNAIRE	CALIPH
				SWEET BRIAR (XX)
			SEINE (XX)	RIVER PRINCE
				FRENCH PARTRIDGE
		PENNYWORT	TOP WALK (XX)	CONCERTO
				PHALARA'S FIRST
			LUCKY PENNY	PENANCE
				LUCKY GIRL

KEY:

XX = THOROUGHBRED

HOLST = HOLSTEIN

OLD = OLDENBERG

TRAK = TRAKEHNER

THE BIRTH OF A CHAMPION

Milton's arrival in the world late one night in April 1977 was unspectacular. He was the first foal of a grey mare called Epauletta. The birth was without complications and the following day the little dark grey colt was turned out with his mother in the paddocks.

Epauletta and the colt's sire, Marius, were owned by John Harding-Rolls, a keen horseman who had long nursed an ambition to breed horses specifically to go show jumping. At the time this was an almost unheard of concept in Britain where, in marked contrast to continental countries such as Germany, France, Holland and Belgium, competition horses have until very recently always been produced more by accident than intent.

Aided by well-known professional horseman Fergus Graham, John Harding-Rolls had formed his own stud in order to attempt to establish tried and tested jumping lines. He continues his quest to the present day at the Marius-Milton Stud, Stratton Audley, in Oxfordshire.

It is John Harding-Rolls who can claim the credit for setting in motion the train of events which produced Milton. In the summer of 1970 he acquired a half-bred mare called Pennywort for Fergus Graham's Dutch-born wife, Paula, to ride. That October at the Horse of the Year Show the mare confirmed her potential by winning the Foxhunter Championship, the premier nation-wide competition for novice horses.

Pennywort was subsequently put in foal to the stallion owned by Fergus and Paula Graham, Any Questions, a grey seven-parts Thoroughbred horse who had proved himself a good all-round performer. He had show jumped, won in the dressage arena and in horse trials and had been regularly hunted. The small amount of non-Thoroughbred blood in his veins had come from his grandsire Caliph, who was by the quality Arabian Shagya Basa, another performance-tested horse who won cross-country endurance tests (50 miles for five days) for Arabians. Pennywort's first foal did not survive, but with better luck at the second attempt, the resulting grey filly was named Epauletta, after Paula Graham.

Meanwhile, Pennywort's owner asked Fergus to look out for a suitable stallion for his stud. He was advised to acquire a horse called Middle Road, so named because he was said to be by the well-known Irish sire, Middle Temple, out of a Connemara mare. Although he felt that there was little in the stallion's appearance to suggest that he was actually sired by Middle Temple, John Harding-Rolls nevertheless decided to buy him.

Despite his fairly small stature – he stood only 16hh – the stallion was well proportioned and he quickly proved that he had plenty of jumping ability. Caroline

Bradley, who would ride a number of horses for John Harding-Rolls over the next decade or so, found that the stallion had superb natural balance and an ideal temperament for the sport of show jumping. Although he was an entire and was used at stud throughout his international career, he was a steady, sensible character, travelled well and never misbehaved in company.

Caroline qualified him for the 1973 Foxhunter Final at Wembley and it was while he was there that his true identity came to light. He was recognised by several people as a Dutch Warmblood called Marius, who had been imported into Britain as a three-year-old. In due course he was re-registered with the British Show Jumping Association under his original name. His pedigree has some impressive bloodlines, including Trakehner, Oldenburg and Holstein, and there is the refining influence of the Thoroughbred via his sire, Marco Polo, who was by Poet out of a Trakehner mare.

In 1976, when she was three, Epauletta was covered by Marius. The result was a colt which John Harding-Rolls aptly called Marius Silver Jubilee. Later, under different ownership, his name would be changed to Milton. Epauletta was subsequently show jumped under the name Aston Answer, and eventually went to Belgium as a brood mare; Marius produced a number of good performance horses from other mares before his death at the end of 1986. Sadly there are no full brothers or sisters to Milton. Produced as he was from two proven performance bloodlines, Marius Silver Jubilee would, it was hoped, demonstrate that breeding show jumpers by selection was a viable proposition, though no one involved could have dreamt that the little colt would turn out to be one horse in a million.

However, while there can be no indication at so early an age that a horse is going to perform exceptionally well over fences, character traits do soon manifest themselves and it was not long before Marius Silver Jubilee started showing the boisterous character that would later earn him some not altogether complimentary nicknames.

Martin Driscoll, who worked as a travelling lad at the stud, and who was present when Epauletta dropped her foal, recalls the colt as a yearling: 'We had a blacksmith who stood about 6ft 6in and I remember Marius Silver Jubilee, as he was then, standing up and planting both front feet on his shoulders when he came to trim his feet!'

Although he had his dam's colouring, it would become obvious that Milton had inherited a great deal, some good, some bad, from his sire: a slight thickness in his wind (Marius suffered all his life from asthma); a tendency to put on too much weight and the concurrent necessity for strict dieting; and, on the plus side, an exceptionally keen interest in everything going on around him. Marius, Caroline once said, would have been quite happy marching along in the middle of the band if there was a parade in the arena. Quite evidently it was from the Dutch stallion that Milton acquired his penchant for playing to the crowd.

However, when it comes to jumping, the question that the experts always come back to is: where did he get his supreme ability? Marius was certainly a talented

individual, but he did not possess anywhere near the scope of his son. And while Epauletta was a careful jumper with a good temperament, she did not exactly set the world of show jumping on fire.

Quite where Milton's incredible powers came from is something of an enigma. Is he a one-off, a fluke result of an admittedly well-planned mating? Or, was there some special chemistry in the mating of Marius and Epauletta and, had there been more progeny, would we now be watching other, equally talented horses, in the world's jumping arenas? Those will forever remain tantalising, unanswerable questions.

CHAPTER 2

MILTON AND THE BRADLEYS

Milton came into Doreen and Tom Bradley's lives through their younger daughter Caroline who, at the time of her tragic death in 1983, was widely considered the world's leading woman show jumper. Natural talent, painstakingly perfected through unflagging dedication and an unsurpassed capacity for sheer hard graft, had taken her to the top of the tree in a sport traditionally dominated by men. David Broome once said of her, 'I don't know anyone in show jumping who would deny her anything because she is such a fighter and works so hard.'

A regular member of the British team, she had over her 17 years on the international circuit acquired an enviable and richly deserved reputation as a brilliant producer of young horses. Her skill at seeking out and nurturing equine talent was second to none.

Milton was bought as a six-month-old foal because she liked both the way he looked and the way he was bred. She paid a thousand pounds for him. By the time he was six she already felt that he had exceptional ability. Here, she sensed, was her next, earnestly hoped-for championship horse, a worthy successor to her previous horse, Tigre. She had lost the ride on the latter – whom she had previously owned jointly with Midlands businessman Donald Bannocks – in 1981, after many months of stressful and ultimately fruitless negotiations. But Milton was hers and hers alone. His presence in her yard would surely make up for all the heartache over Tigre. At the start of the 1983 season she had no reason to look into the years ahead with anything but optimism. Then fate intervened in no uncertain terms, as it was to do several times during Milton's rise to fame. A few months later Caroline was gone and suddenly Milton's future lay in the hands of her bewildered and grieving parents.

Caroline and her sister Judith, older by four years, inherited their love of horses from their mother, Doreen. Born in Ireland, where horses have always been a way of life rather than a mere recreation, Doreen had a father who farmed, a mother whose family kept racehorses and an uncle who was a master of foxhounds. Little wonder then, that she grew up with an innate love of riding, hunting and the countryside. Her mother, she recalls, always used to say that when a horse died, the family mourned; when a relative died, they did not.

Doreen's family left Ireland when she was still very young. However, there was no question of the move curtailing such important activities as riding and hunting. With the family farm now in Northamptonshire, they simply switched their allegiance to the Bicester Hunt.

On the other hand Caroline's father, Tom Bradley, is the first to admit that he had no interest whatsoever in things equestrian, finding a cricket bat and a rugger ball much more to his liking than a saddle and bridle. He did, however, share Doreen's affinity with country life. A chartered surveyor by profession, he worked with the Land Commission and later as a County Land Agent.

As Doreen succinctly puts it, 'If Tom wanted anything to do with me, he had to tag along with the horses.' And tag along he did, and to his considerable astonishment, found himself duly promoted to the position of head stable lad. Little could he have suspected when he joined Doreen in matrimony that he was destined to find personal fame in the equestrian world.

When Doreen and Tom married in 1940 they set up home at Tyringham, on the borders of Northamptonshire and Buckinghamshire. Judith, born during 1942, and Caroline, who followed in April 1946, had scarcely arrived in the world before the rhythmic clip-clop of ponies' hooves was drumming in their ears. 'When Judith arrived there was a war on and I didn't so much push a pram as drive a pony and trap. I used to wrap the little bundle up, put it in the trap and that was that.'

Like so many children in a similar environment, the girls literally grew up with ponies. They were put in the saddle before they could walk, in their case on Doreen's little driving pony. Before the war this pony had been in a circus and would still perform tricks such as standing on a barrel. His equable temperament made him an ideal introduction to the equine world for two small girls.

By the time she was four Caroline had grasped the basics of balance, steering and braking, and would be found arranging sticks on the ground to jump over. There was also the influence of her mother's inherent love of National Hunt racing, which meant that the girls 'cut their teeth on racecards — they used to ride their ponies up and down the drive like mad things.'

With a young family to bring up the Bradleys could not afford to keep a horse for Doreen to hunt, but she continued to ride whenever she could, helping to exercise the girls' bigger ponies and, when the girls were older, their horses. Only when she had to have a replacement hip operation and was told to 'play golf' instead did she reluctantly hang up her boots.

The fulcrum for the girls' early riding experience was the Pony Club. This renowned organisation, founded in 1929 to encourage children to enjoy horse sports and to receive skilled instruction, is the largest association of riders in the world, with branches in many English-speaking countries outside the United Kingdom. Hundreds of thousands of youngsters have, like the Bradleys, benefited from the no-nonsense grounding provided at Pony Club camps, rallies and competitions where everyone is encouraged to have fun, while at the same time learning to take seriously the responsibilities of caring for their ponies. Countless present-day international riders, John Whitaker among them, gained their early equestrian experience with the Pony Club, which welcomes everyone, rich and poor alike.

The Bradley girls by no means came into the former category and rarely had smart, showy ponies to ride. Mostly they were the same sort of animals that their mother had owned as a child, acquired as unbroken three-year-olds and costing around the £20 mark. Doreen undertook the breaking-in of these ponies herself, all that is except the mouthing process. This is a highly skilled and crucial part of a horse's early training, which teaches him to accept a bit in his mouth, without which more advanced schooling is impossible. Done well, mouthing can make a horse or pony a happy individual and a joy to ride; done badly or hurriedly, it can turn him into a discontented, difficult and potentially dangerous liability for the rest of his life.

Doreen Bradley always preferred to have a good local horseman carry out this part of her ponies' education. Then, after the ponies were mouthed, she spent hours walking them out on long reins to teach them to go forward, turn and stop when requested and generally make them as safe as possible for the girls to ride. For all that, the Bradley girls were not always mounted on patent safeties. Early on, their mother remembers, they had 'an 11-hand thing that hadn't any breaks and very little steering', followed by 'an ignorant 12.2' and, much later, a 'wild four-year-old hunter, a really nappy horse when we bought it'. The pony which more than any other set Caroline up was a brilliant cross-country performer called Just Jimmy. 'He was a hot pony, but very good. He hunted, hunter trialled, Pony Clubbed, jumped, everything.' All of it invaluable experience for two girls who would eventually both earn their living in the horse world: Judith in racing, Caroline in show jumping.

As Caroline progressed through Pony Club activities, competing in hunter trials, in horse trials and riding to hounds, it became obvious to those with a keen eye that here was more than an ordinary talent. The late Dorian Williams, a fine judge of both horse and rider, recalled that when he first saw her riding at the Grafton Hunt Pony Club as early as 1955, he was so impressed that he immediately enquired who she was. Dorian followed her subsequent career with keen interest. Writing in 1970 about the wealth of talent among Britain's women riders – in marked contrast to most other countries – he cited the achievements of the current established stars adding, with consummate prescience, that 'Caroline Bradley may turn out to be the best of all. Certainly she has succeeded on far more horses, many of them far from easy rides and frequently difficult in temperament.' Prophetic words indeed.

Doreen Bradley cannot recall there being a precise moment when her daughter decided on a career as a show jumper or indeed that she ever entertained any childhood ambitions in that direction. Caroline had never been on the junior jumping circuit, in its way as professional as the senior equivalent. It was an unfamiliar scene to the Bradleys. Caroline's preference had always been cross-country riding and as a member of the Pony Club, she had evented. She had been a member of many Pony Club teams, where show jumping had featured among the activities, but not to the exclusion of all else. In Caroline's case, specialising in jumping merely came about as a natural progression through working with horses, bringing on youngsters and taking them to little local competitions as part of their education. Only gradually, from the time she started riding her sister's horse, Nikomis, as a junior associate member of the British Show Jumping Association, and later her own mare Justina, was she pointed in the direction of the sport.

MILTON TAKING HIS USUAL KEEN INTEREST IN THINGS AROUND HIM – OR PERHAPS HE HAS SIMPLY SEEN THE FEED BUCKET?

Tom Bradley had always insisted that he did not mind his daughter 'sticking with horses' provided she first trained for a profession. There was no question of her leaving school, as so many girls do, at sixteen, to try to scrape a living in the horse world. Accordingly, Caroline continued with her studies until she was eighteen, passing her A levels and successfully applying for a place at Bedford College to study

training. She swam well, played a good game of tennis and squash and was a junior international hockey player. There was nothing to prevent her becoming a first-class PE instructor – except her love of horses.

As the time came nearer for her to leave school she began to put pressure on her father, saying she did not really want to go to college and that she would only be keeping somebody else out. Then fate, on this occasion clearly on her side, took a hand. The college said they could quite happily hold the place for her until she was 21. 'I've got to make it by the time I'm 21 then, haven't I?' was her response. Her father capitulated, Caroline jubilantly put aside all immediate thoughts of becoming a PE instructor and in no time at all had packed her riding gear and moved down to Lars Sederholm's equestrian training centre at Waterstock, in Oxfordshire.

She had already spent part of her school holidays taking instruction from this gifted Swedish-born horseman and now she was to learn in no uncertain terms just how much hard work was required for a rider to graduate to top-level competition. Previously she had ridden for fun. Now she was out to show that she had the talent and perseverance to make a living from horses. During 18 months' concentrated work at Waterstock she proved that she was more than equal to the challenge.

Under Lars' supervision she buckled down to the prime task of improving her riding skills sufficiently to enable her to train and bring on young horses to the point where they could compete successfully. Ironing out her basic faults entailed hours and hours of riding with her arms behind her back, and a stick pushed through them to keep her shoulders back. In her book *Show Jumping With Caroline Bradley* (Pelham Books, 1981), she remembers:

> To make me use my back and seat I had masses and masses of lessons where I was lunged without reins or stirrups over one or two fences on a circle . . . although I could just about manage to sit one or two fences, eventually I would fly straight on while the horse was still going on the circle. I had raw, bleeding knees and seemed to ache permanently, but it taught me a lot.

As her own ability improved she began to spend more and more time schooling young horses, both her own and those belonging to Lars. Never one to shirk hard work, she threw herself into the daily routine of training on the flat, mastering the art of keeping half a ton of horse balanced and in the right outline to jump a fence with the minimum amount of effort. Done correctly, it all looks so easy; in reality it is the result of sheer hard slog.

Caroline was to demonstrate the excellence of her all-round horsemanship a few years later when in 1969 she rode in the world's toughest three-day event at Badminton – arguably the greatest overall test of competitive riding anywhere – finishing in a very creditable 16th place on Lars Sederholm's horse Alpaca. The winner was Richard Walker, another protégé of the Swedish master. While riding for Lars, Caroline was also entrusted with jumping Doublet – the horse on which Princess Anne was to win the European Three-Day Event Championship in 1971.

When she first went to Waterstock Caroline was still too young to have an HGV licence so her parents would go down whenever she needed a driver and ferry her around the national show circuit, her mother invariably taking the wheel of the horsebox. It was not long, Doreen recalls, before her daughter began to catch the eye of the establishment:

> I remember standing in the crowd at Richmond and in front of me were David Barker and, as I remember, Andrew Massarella. Caroline had been riding some horses of Lars' and they had been going well and I heard Andrew say, "That's a good girl" – the sort of remark that makes you prick up your ears. David said, "She could have my brown horse but she's tied to Lars Sederholm, isn't she?" and I said, Oh no she isn't, she just happens to be based there.

In due course she was indeed given the ride on the 'brown horse', Robert Hanson's Franco, who had helped David Barker win the 1962 men's European Championship and had been in many Nations Cup teams. A fearless horse and a strong puller, Franco settled down well in Caroline's sympathetic hands.

Four months after her 20th birthday she confirmed the opinion of the ringside experts. Invited to make her debut with the British team, she took a Russian-bred horse called Ivanovitch, who had cost her parents all of £50, to the 1966 Royal Dublin Show, where she won two speed classes and was consistently well placed throughout the show. As far as her future was concerned, the die was cast.

The deadline of her 21st birthday came and went. There was now no question of putting her equestrian career on hold to go to college. Caroline had proved that there was a place for her in the world of international show jumping and for the next 17 years she was to carry the British flag with distinction. Riding Franco, she made her first ever Nations Cup appearance in Olsztyn, Poland, in June 1967. She and her team-mates, John Kidd, Simon Rodgerson and John Baillie, rode to victory over a strong West German team and a week later Caroline made it two-out-of-two when Franco jumped the only double clear in Leipzig to lead the British squad to another fine Cup win. Later in the year she was selected to go on the American Fall Circuit, to compete in the Nations Cup in New York and Toronto. She and Franco continued their impressive form by finishing as runners-up to Harvey Smith and O'Malley in the Grand Prix at the former and winning the Civilian Open Championship at the latter.

By the early 70's Caroline was firmly established as one of the world's top women riders and when the selectors asked if Wood Nymph, a mare she was riding with notable success, would be available for the 1972 Olympics in Munich she naturally agreed, assuming she was included in the invitation. However, it turned out that the mare was being considered as a possible partner for two of the top men riders, David Broome and Peter Robeson. Wood Nymph did not go well for either of them and Caroline was greatly upset watching them attempt to form a partnership with her. In the event David rode Manhattan at the Games and Peter Robeson was omitted from the team. It was after this episode that Caroline said to her mother, 'No horse of mine will ever go to the Olympics.' A prophetic statement, which was to have considerable bearing on Milton's career.

The following year Caroline's chances of competing in the Olympics were, as it happened, entirely wiped out. In a vain attempt to bring riders, and other athletes, competing at Olympic level nearer to the original Olympic ideal of true amateurism, moves were afoot to amend the rules governing amateurs and professionals. Caroline, along with a number of other top British riders, was reclassified as a professional by her national federation, the British Show Jumping Association, because she rode horses for other people. Her appeal against the decision, based on the fact that she was receiving no payment for riding other owners' horses, was unsuccessful.

Ironically, the zeal with which Britain sorted out its 'amateurs' and 'professionals' was not imitated by most other leading equestrian nations with the result that for a number of years the British jumping team was at a distinct disadvantage at the Olympic Games. The whole unsatisfactory situation was not resolved until 1987 when riders formerly forced to turn professional were allowed to revert to 'competitor' (previously known as 'amateur') status. That, under new International Olympic Committee rules, made them once more eligible for the Games but, as it turned out, was too late to be of any benefit to Caroline.

From 1973 onwards she put the Olympics firmly out of her mind and concentrated on other goals. By this time she had become acquainted with John Harding-Rolls, one of the two people who was to play a dominant role as a supplier of horses during her career – the other being the renowned German rider and breeder of competition horses, Paul Schockemöhle. She rode a total of 16 horses for John Harding-Rolls during their long association and bought a number of youngsters from his stud.

He had asked her to ride his recently acquired stallion Middle Road (later to be renamed Marius) and Caroline qualified him for the 1973 Foxhunter Championship at Wembley, which he was unlucky not to win. In the final jump-off Caroline, like the preceding rider, jumped a fence which was not part of the shortened course, but which apparently had not been flagged to warn riders to that effect. It was not until after Marius had jumped that the first rider was eliminated, and then, of course, Caroline was eliminated, too.

In the years ahead, Marius was to make up handsomely for the disappointment of not winning that much coveted Foxhunter title. He became a regular and valuable member of the British team and because, unlike some stallions, he had such a marvellous temperament, he was able to combine stud duties and a show jumping career with no problem whatsoever. Caroline found that he could be switched from covering mares at home to jumping in an international arena with no fear that he would misbehave, despite the close presence of attractive equine ladies.

During 1973 Caroline had ridden True Lass and another good horse, New Yorker, in the Ladies' European Championship in Vienna, finishing runner-up to Ann Moore and Psalm. The following year she teamed up True Lass with Middle Road, as he was still known at the time, for what turned out to be the last running of a separate World Championship for women (from 1975 onwards both European and World titles became open to men and women). Caroline finished equal third with the Canadian Barbara Simpson Kerr though in the official records she is credited

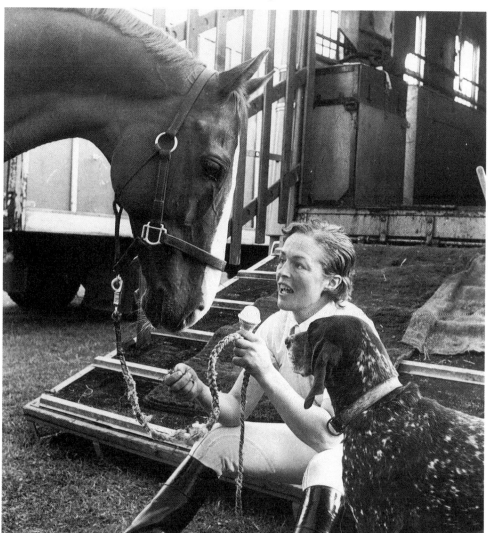

CAROLINE BRADLEY AND FRIENDS. A SKILFUL PRODUCER OF YOUNG HORSES, CAROLINE BOUGHT MILTON AS A FOAL AND SET HIM ON THE PATH TO INTERNATIONAL FAME, BEFORE HER PREMATURE DEATH IN 1983

with fourth position. This is because the placings were decided not by a jump-off but by the best placings in the three qualifying competitions and the Canadian had two marginally better placings than Caroline.

The next European Championships were limited to amateurs only, which precluded Caroline's participation, and Marius never did win a championship medal. He nevertheless gave Caroline some notable successes, among them the 1978 Queen Elizabeth II Cup at the Royal International (in which he had been runner-up the previous year) and the first Volvo World Cup qualifying round to be held on British soil, at the Birmingham show in the spring of 1979. He was also in five winning Nations Cup teams, in Paris, Geneva (twice), Hickstead and Calgary. And, in the midst of this busy international career, he made his biggest contribution of all to British show jumping: he sired Milton.

Over the years, her mother recalls, Caroline bought a lot of young horses from John Harding-Rolls, including several sired by Marius. Despite having had many more horses from Paul Schockemöhle, she actually preferred the Marius youngsters. Caroline picked out Milton as a six-month-old foal, though her mother warns against getting too carried away in crediting her with uncanny foresight over this particular purchase: 'It wasn't unusual for her to buy horses from John Harding-Rolls that young – she had a lot before Milton and a lot after.' But Caroline did have a firm belief that here was a horse with the right bloodlines to go show jumping:

> It was the Thoroughbred blood in Any Questions' pedigree that particularly appealed to her and helped make her decide to buy Marius Silver Jubilee as he was then known. She always preferred blood horses like Franco to the rather common, heavier types.

In due course the son of Marius joined Caroline's other guests at The Cedars, in the Warwickshire village of Priors Marston. This was the home which the Bradleys had bought when their daughter's career began to develop, and the aquisition of more horses made it imperative for her to have more land. Caroline, who liked her horses to have simple names – 'ones that show secretaries could spell' – renamed her new acquisition Milton, after a nearby Northamptonshire village. It was a practice she often employed, at various times jumping horses with names such as Stockton, Hinton, Kingston, Leighton and Compton.

Although he had inherited his dam's colouring, Milton's main personality traits seem to have come from his sire. Like Marius he was a bouncy youngster and like Marius he had, and still has, a Houdini-like gift for unfastening gates and stable doors, not to mention a talent for removing his rugs and destroying rollers, the latter simply by blowing out his stomach and bursting them. He was also such a bossy individual that the girl grooms nicknamed him 'Hitler'.

Caroline used to say that breaking-in horses was not her speciality, though she was in fact perfectly competent at it. However, as a rider on the international circuit she felt she had insufficient time to devote to this all-important time in a horse's education. It is not a job that should be hurried, particularly if the horse is a bit of a character and inclined to be strong and boisterous, and so Milton was sent away to be broken-in by Yorkshire farmer Bill Brown, who over the years broke-in most of her youngsters. As in most walks of life, the backroom boys of the horse world rarely receive the acclaim they deserve, yet it is those people like Bill Brown with skill, patience and experience, who help mould a potentially difficult young horse into a world beater. He has broken-in horses all his life, racehorses as well as jumpers and admitted that 'Milton was a bit of a handful to begin with. He stayed with us for almost a year. Ian, one of my boys, who later went to work for Caroline for six months, used to ride him.'

Mr Brown remembers Caroline arriving at his stables one day with a carload of people. Milton was being ridden in the yard and he asked her if she would like to sit on him. In her customary self-effacing way, Caroline declined, but as soon as everyone had disappeared into the house she did get up on him. Sadly, there is no record of the moment.

During Milton's first few years of exuberant life, Caroline's international jumping career was at its zenith, largely because she had by now established a wonderful partnership with Tigre. When she first saw the grey Hannoverian gelding he was already well known to some of the leading continental riders, several of whom had tried him and rejected him, among them Johann Heins and Gerd Wiltfang. Caroline admitted later that she was not instantly convinced about him: he was green, spooky and more interested in things around him than in work. But she did feel that the horse had potential and accordingly persuaded Donald Bannocks, who was interested in owning a good show jumper, to put up a major part of the purchase price. Later Caroline owned a half-share in the horse.

For two years the partnership of Caroline and Tigre was one of the strongest anywhere in the world. In the 1978 World Championships in Aachen, where Caroline was the only woman rider in a field of 53, they jumped a double-clear round in the Nations Cup, except for a quarter of a time fault, clinching the team gold medal for Britain and only narrowly missed qualifying for the 'change-horse' individual final. 12 months later they helped Britain win the team gold in the European Championships in Rotterdam. They were in winning Nations Cup teams at Hickstead (twice), Calgary and Paris, and took, among other big prizes, the Grand Prix in Nice and then Calgary.

In recognition of her contribution to the equestrian world Caroline was awarded the MBE in 1980. But by the time of that year's Royal International Horse Show the storm clouds were gathering. Donald Bannocks had decided to put Tigre up for sale by sealed tender and even as she was winning her second Queen Elizabeth II

Cup, this time with the big grey, Caroline knew there was a real possibility that she would lose the ride on her best horse. For a while Mr Bannocks, having bought Caroline's share from her, retained sole ownership of the horse. Caroline continued to ride him, though inevitably without the same feeling of security, and he finished the 1980 season as the top British prize-money winner at international level.

Things began to look brighter when Caroline signed a sponsorship contract at the end of the year with Tricentrol. The deal, taking effect from 1981, covered her young, up-and-coming horses and she undertook to have ten jumping with the Tricentrol (later Trimoco) prefix. Then came the bombshell. At the beginning of 1981 Tigre, her one top horse, was suddenly removed from her yard and subsequently sold.

It was a bitter blow but typically Caroline picked herself up, dusted herself down and began setting about the arduous task of building up a new string of Grade A horses in the hope of discovering another star. It was, she said, bred in her to resent paying high prices for horses. She preferred to keep her eyes open and to watch out for the right breeding. She favoured certain bloodlines and her assessment of Milton's was to prove absolutely correct. That, together with her own outstanding gifts at giving the right basic training, is what put Milton on the path to becoming a super champion.

Caroline had always enjoyed producing young horses. She once told Pamela MacGregor-Morris, of *The Times* (*Horse and Rider Yearbook 1979*, Macdonald and Jane's 1979)

> I love riding young horses until they can jump a novice course easily, but I find it boring to take them to Grade A because it takes so long. Basically I love the really young horses and I love the older horses.

With Milton, it was not so much a case of the time it took to get to Grade A but of how to prevent him getting there too soon for his own good. As was her custom, Caroline took him very quietly through the novice competition stage as a five and six year old. Unfortunately, few photographs exist of him from that period. Milton was only one amongst many and riders tend not to spend money on too many pictures of their novices, explains Doreen, of the family's lack of a comprehensive record. He may have been one amongst many, but one thing which Caroline said early on in Milton's novice career sticks in her mother's memory: 'He's so difficult to ride because anything I ask him to jump, he will jump; any pressure I give him, he just comes up higher.' It was, of course, the mark of a very good horse indeed.

Doreen also clearly recalls a disastrous occasion when he failed to win a foxhunter regional final:

> It was my fault because I was watching and had parked my car at the ringside, right between the two parts of the combination. Milton was going beautifully

until he reached the combination. Then he suddenly saw my bright yellow car, spooked and ran out. Caroline hardly spoke to me for two days. But I think she knew in her heart of hearts that he didn't really **need** to win a Foxhunter because every time she took him out he kept winning and he was simply upgrading too quickly.

In 1982 Milton, still at the very novice stage, was campaigned like all Caroline's 'babies' with great care. He was never rushed nor asked to follow a rigid schedule. Her general approach was to give her horses a few low-level competitions as four-year-olds, then turn them out in the field, before bringing them back up into regular work and competition during the summer of their fifth year. She reckoned to have a good idea by the time they were six whether they were going to be just average or rather more than that. By 1983, her mother says, Caroline had no doubt that in Milton she had a special horse.

In the summer of 1982 she had taken him to his first Royal International Horse Show. He was qualified for the Grade C Championship and jumped a double-clear round. He did not win because Caroline, ever mindful of the need to hasten slowly with young horses, did not push him against the clock. No one was more aware of the dangers of asking a talented youngster to do too much too soon, to force them into bad habits or simply make them out of love with the game.

Steve Hadley, who was to become Milton's next partner, recalls that 'he had been noticed by a number of people as a five-year-old. I remember when he jumped those two clear rounds at the Royal International someone saying "Caroline's not rushing him because she thinks a lot of him".'

Milton was one of the horses that Caroline loaded on the lorry on Wednesday, June 1 1983, the fateful day that was to shake the show jumping world. Her destination was the two-day Suffolk County Show at Ipswich where the horse she jumped, Rubber Ball, in the Top Score competition, eventually finished second. As she dismounted from him in the collecting ring she told her groom that she was not feeling well. Suddenly she collapsed. An ambulance was summoned, but she died of heart failure on the way to hospital. She was 37.

Those who knew her were convinced that it was stress and overwork which were the principle causes of her premature death. A perfectionist in all she did, she had always found it difficult to delegate and would work punishingly long hours to satisfy herself of the well-being of her horses. Ron Longford, the chiropractor, who figures later on in the Milton story, recalls that no matter how late he called at her yard to look at a horse's back or leg, he would always find Caroline at work. And it was not just the schooling, riding and care of such a large string; there was also the mountain of paperwork involved in the running of a jumping yard, which often kept her awake into the early hours of the morning; plus the hours and hours spent at the wheel of her horsebox, both in Britain and on the Continent. She had good girls working for her but always felt she must check on every detail herself.

Ironically, in her time she had survived some dreadful injuries. As a teenager she suffered severe spleen and liver damage when one of her horses kicked her; some years later her mother found her laid out on the paving stones outside the house with a fractured skull; at one time a broken knee threatened her whole riding future. And, in common with all riders, there had been the usual quota of crunching falls. John Harding-Rolls recalled an occasion when she had a crashing fall at Aldershot from one of his novices. On the two following days she was at Burley-on-the-Hill riding for him, 'when her head must have been throbbing terribly – yet she went out and won two classes.' Tough as she was, ultimately the sport she loved simply wore her out.

As the news of her death began to sink in, so the tributes flowed, all of them touching on the same theme.

> Her great talent was her ability to ride all sorts of horses – she could get on anything and ride it. And she was the hardest working person in the world
>
> (David Broome)

> She was the most dedicated show jumper I've known – she lived for horses. She got to the top because she was prepared to put the work in and because she was so dedicated
>
>   (Derek Ricketts, like David a member of the 1978 World Championship team)

> Caroline's death has been just about as bitter a blow as a man can sustain. She was probably the most hard working, dedicated, courageous person that I have ever had the good fortune to know
>
> (John Harding-Rolls)

> She was perhaps the hardest working and most dedicated person that I have met
>
> (Roger Smith, Chairman of her sponsors, Trimoco)

Her funeral service, held in St Leonard's, the 16th century parish church of her home village, Priors Marston, had to be relayed to an overflowing congregation outside. The British jumping team, which should have been on its way to the Nations Cup in Paris, insisted on taking a later flight so that they could attend. Her long-time associate Paul Schockemöhle flew over from Germany.

Milton and the 28 other horses in her yard at the time of her death were suddenly left high and dry, like the crew of a ship bereft of its captain.

CHAPTER 3

THE DARK DAYS

The suddenness of Caroline's death and the responsibility of coping with a stable full of fit horses left her parents in a state of shock and bewilderment. They felt they needed a month or so to take stock of things before they decided what to do, so they told the girls to run things down gradually, and just keep the horses fed and exercised.

To begin with the Bradleys entertained thoughts of continuing to run things themselves: 'It was a lovely yard and we felt we would have liked to have kept it going in some way or other.' There was even a talented rider available at the time who might well have made a suitable 'stable jockey', though no approach was ever actually made to the person concerned. Friends and acquaintances were quick in coming up with suggestions, some of which, Doreen felt, were rather less than altruistic. It was then that they realised they had to pull themselves together, look at the books and see how they could work things out.

A lot of the horses simply went back to their owners, but Caroline had owned Milton outright. The Bradleys decided to ring John Whitaker and ask if he would be interested in having him. They chose John, Doreen explained, because Caroline had always liked his riding and his general approach to horses, and they felt she would have approved of his having the youngster of whom she thought so highly.

John said he would like to go down to Warwickshire to try him. But as luck would have it he was about to set off from his Yorkshire stables with a lorry load of horses to compete on the Scottish circuit. He hoped that he would be able to try the horse when he returned from this trip a couple of weeks later. However, by the time he got back he found that the Bradleys had made other arrangements.

Feeling that things were beginning to get on top of them, they decided not to wait for John's return but to send the remaining horses, including Milton, to their near neighbour Steve Hadley who, after Caroline's death, had offered to help in any way he could should they wish to call on him. Milton, Rubber Ball, Granita, Kingston, Hypericum and Marco were duly installed at Steve's yard at Chadshunt, near Kineton, and he competed with them under the Trimoco banner until the end of 1983.

Steve had been competing internationally for many years and had ridden some good horses. He had qualified for that year's World Cup Final in Vienna with his reliable mare Sunorra. But he felt that Milton was in a different class from other horses he had ridden as soon as he started jumping him. It was, he said, simply the feeling he gave you when he came off the ground. He was still Grade B at the time and not being asked to jump big fences, but his new rider sensed the remarkable potential within that athletic frame. His one failing as a youngster, Steve said, was his tendency to dangle his front legs over a fence. He recalled seeing Caroline jumping him at Balsall Common when he hit five fences because of this failure to fold up his forelegs. Such carelessness can only be cured through schooling, and it is a tribute to the correctness of Caroline's groundwork that Milton overcame the habit. Steve also says that the grey was always a bit 'loopy'. He could 'leap sideways 20 yards' when he saw something to spook at.

For the first few months Steve took Milton to shows on the outdoor circuit. He jumped clear rounds with great regularity and it was not long before he became Grade A. Then he was given a month off and the plan was to take him to the Christmas show at Olympia where Steve felt that, although he was still only six, he would cope well enough with the small classes. As it turned out Milton neither reached Olympia that time nor was seen again in a jumping arena for the best part of two years.

Steve had gone abroad to compete. While he was away Milton was being spruced up ready for his trip to London. He was not being clipped out, merely having his heels trimmed, but what has proved to be a life-long aversion to clippers manifested itself that day in no uncertain terms, and put him on the injured list. No one knows to this day exactly what happened. He suddenly took it into his head to rear up and strike out, and when he came down to earth again he had sustained a cut on his near foreleg. It might have been caused by the clipper blades or it could have been simply that he struck into himself – no one could say for sure.

Although the injury appeared not to be particularly serious Milton was not quite sound. The Bradleys decided to have him examined by Geoffrey Braine, a Gloucestershire veterinary surgeon whose opinion Caroline had always valued highly. The news was bad: he diagnosed tendon damage. The recommended treatment was a split tendon operation, in which the tendon fibres are separated, a process which encourages stronger growth during healing. Tendon injuries always require a long period of rest if the horse is be totally sound afterwards and in Milton's case Geoffrey Braine suggested at least a year off, saying that 18 months would be even better.

Steve Hadley had noticed that Milton did not seem to be clear in his wind – a defect he had inherited from his sire, Marius – so it was decided at the same time to have him Hobdayed. This operation, named after its pioneer, the distinguished veterinary surgeon Sir Frederick Hobday (1870-1939) relieves problems caused by the paralysis of muscles controlling the larynx. The idea is to allow a free passage of air into the horse's lungs by attempting, through surgery, to get the vocal folds to adhere to the side of the larynx. This prevents the paralysed chord from being sucked into the airway when the horse breathes in. When Milton had undergone his operations, he went home to Priors Marston to recuperate and Steve paid regular visits to check on his progress.

Meanwhile the Bradleys, no longer needing Caroline's extensive stabling and schooling facilities, decided to sell The Cedars and move to their present home on the other side of the village. In due course, during the winter of 1984, the time came to move Milton too. Because of his long lay-off from work it was a task the Bradleys approached with well-founded anxiety. Doreen remembers the experience to this day: 'It was very snowy and we had a fair idea he'd be a lunatic. You should have seen the two of us walking up the road with our wild grey animal.'

Mission accomplished, thankfully without damage to horse or humans, Milton was turned out with an old horse for company in the field adjoining the Bradleys' new house. Roaming about in this field, set on a hill, helped strengthen him up. Doreen Bradley knew full well the value of hillwork. Indeed, she believes that one of the reasons why Milton is such a fit, sound horse is because, throughout his jumping career, he has always had hills to run on, first in Warwickshire and then at John Whitaker's home in Yorkshire. Not that Milton always thought his field the most entertaining place to be. When he was bored he would let himself out and take a turn in the garden, a habit which did not exactly endear him to his owners.

On January 30, 1985, he was moved to the neighbouring village of Priors Hardwick to be treated by renowned chiropractor Ron Longford. There was still heat in the injured leg and Ron recalls that the Bradleys were very upset, and fairly pessimistic about the chances of Milton ever being fit again to compete. He was based at Evelyn England's livery yard and Ron started a course of ultra-sonic treatment.

Milton was no stranger to Ron Longford, who had known the horse as 'Robin' when Milton was a three-year-old. Ron paid regular visits to Caroline's yard to treat her competition horses. Although he did break a window in his stable on arrival, Milton was not a bad patient, Ron recalls, and was far less destructive of rugs than his sire, Marius.

After a few weeks, when the heat in his leg had subsided, Milton started gentle work, usually with Evelyn aboard, though occasionally Ron rode him, too. In common with everyone who has had anything to do with him, Ron remembers the grey's spookiness. 'One day he would go past an articulated lorry and not even look at it, the next day he would spook at a blackbird.' On one occasion when he was out exercising with Evelyn he decided to take exception to a piece of corrugated iron which he had seen many times before: he reared up, lost his balance and fell over backwards. Picking himself up he cantered off home, leaving Evelyn to make her own way back. Once again, fortunately, neither party was any the worse for the experience. Not surprisingly, they preferred, if possible, to keep him off the roads, and luckily they had the use of Caroline's old school at The Cedars.

Milton stayed with Ron and Evelyn until 25 May, by which time he was considered fit enough to go back into proper work. Although there was, and still is, a slight thickening at the site of the injury, there was no longer any sign of heat and Milton had remained as sound as a bell under light work. The Bradleys now had to decide anew on the horse's future. They consulted Caroline's old friend and business

MILTON AND HIS GROOM PENNY STEVENS SHARE A QUIET MOMENT DURING THE 1990 WORLD EQUESTRIAN GAMES

associate Paul Schockemöhle. Paul at that time was still competing, and had recently helped set up a deal for John and Michael Whitaker with his own sponsors, the clothing retailers Next. After discussions with Paul, it was decided that Milton should again be offered to John – who accepted and this time there was no hitch. John's box, returning from a trip to Spain where the British team had won the Madrid Nations Cup, stopped on its way north to pick up the grey, and by the beginning of June he was established in his new home.

This time it was Steve Hadley's turn to miss out. Unlike John he had sampled Milton's potential and was naturally disappointed not to have the horse back. On the other hand he was 13 years John's senior and nearing the end of his international

MILTON WITH FRIENDS GAMMON (LEFT) AND DOLLAR GIRL AT JOHN'S YORKSHIRE STABLES

career. Already he was devoting more and more time to two other activities at which he was proving extremely successful, teaching and television commentating. Having Milton at this stage would have meant all the extra hassle of maintaining a back-up string of horses just at the time when he was wanting to cut back on this very aspect of his work. Milton came into his life a decade too late and, he says, in the final analysis, 'I never was that dedicated to competing.'

While no one would ever be foolish enough to welcome a tendon injury, in retrospect the long lay-off from work necessitated by Milton's accident could well be considered a blessing in disguise. For a horse to be capable of winning £500 classes (good money in those days) as a six-year-old, as Milton was, may be very exciting for his connections but it could prove disastrous for the horse. As John says, with a horse who finds jumping relatively easy, there is always the temptation to push on too soon. Such was Milton's ability that he was in grave danger of reaching the top too quickly, before he was fully mature either physically or mentally. In many people's estimation, including the Bradleys, Steve Hadley and John, the fact that the horse was eight before he was able to start serious competition has prolonged his career as a top international horse. John says that in his first seven seasons with him there were only two occasions when he could not jump him when he wanted to. At 15 he was still free of the leg and back troubles which tend to bedevil show jumping horses.

Despite a three-month holiday, after injuring himself in the sticky going at the Pavarotti show in Italy, he still finished the 1991 season as the top money winner with £193,985 to his credit, only marginally less than his tally for the previous year.

CHAPTER 4

A NEW BEGINNING

John Whitaker was approaching his 30th birthday and firmly established as one of the world's top riders when Milton joined his yard in the summer of 1985. Good riders, they say, attract good horses, and if anyone has proved the truth of this maxim it is John. Taught to ride by his mother, Enid, he gained his early competitive experience at local gymkhanas and with the Pony Club. Like Caroline Bradley, he showed such exceptional talent for getting the best from all types of ponies and horses that owners soon began sending him their animals to ride.

His most famous and successful partner before Milton was another great character, Ryan's Son, acquired for him by his future father-in-law, Malcolm Barr. Ryan's Son, with his plain white face and high-spirited kick-back, was, like his grey successor, an instantly recognisable personality on the jumping circuit and adored by the public. John was not yet 21 when he became National Champion with him in 1976 and for the next decade the pair were one of the mainstays of the British team.

They won individual and team silver medals in the 1980 International Show Jumping Festival (staged for the countries which boycotted the Moscow Games); finished equal third in the 1982 World Cup and took a team bronze in the World Championships; were team and individual silver medallists in the 1983 Europeans, and won both the World Cup European League and the Hickstead Derby; helped Britain win the team silver in the 1984 Los Angeles Olympics; and crowned a glorious career with victory in the King George V Gold Cup at the Royal International in 1986.

John could scarcely have been united with Milton at a better time. He had this enormous wealth of experience at championship level behind him and although Ryan's Son was approaching the end of his honourable career John was on the way to building up a strong team of horses to carry on where he left off. They included Hopscotch, team gold and individual bronze medallist in the 1985 Europeans and team silver medallist in the World Championships the following year; the brilliant speed horse San Salvador and the up-and-coming Gammon, of whom John had high hopes. There was no great need to hurry Milton, who was after all still a very inexperienced Grade A horse. Milton, it seems, had his own ideas about that and the speed with which he became the star of the Whitaker stable took John totally by surprise.

Milton, he recalls, was decidedly on the stout side when he arrived at his stables near Upper Cumberworth in West Yorkshire. He is a horse who is inclined to carry a lot of weight at the best of times, and it was a long while since he had been in serious work. As a result he was also pretty unfit, so John decided to spend the first two months riding him on the flat to tone him up and make sure he was strong in his legs.

When he did at last put up a small fence for Milton to pop over he was impressed

with the feel the horse gave him, though experience had taught him to be cautious in his assessment of any new ride:

> It happens a lot: you ride a horse and it feels good, then a couple of months afterwards it's not as good as you expected. So you tend not to build your hopes too high. Milton did feel very very good – but I didn't think at that precise moment we were going to beat the world with him.

John did, however, like the horse's general attitude, his inquisitiveness and his interest in everything going on around him, very much. Even before he embarked on his first trip abroad with him, he had begun to feel that he was 'a bit special'.

A couple of years later John made what has become one of his most famous dead-pan remarks when he was asked by a journalist, 'Is there a big difference between

Ryan's Son and Milton?' and he replied, after a moment's serious reflection, 'Ay ... colour.' John does indeed make riding Milton look as easy as that, but in reality it took time for him to adapt his riding to suit his new partner's unusual jumping style.

To bystanders it seems that Milton jumps in slow motion and this, apparently, is exactly how it feels to his rider. John found that Milton took much longer than most horses to pick up in front of a fence and fold up his forelegs. Normally the cure would be to bring the horse a bit closer to the fence and with slightly more pace. But when John tried this with Milton it made him worse and instead of snapping up his front legs more quickly he would simply twist himself over the fence. The answer was in fact to stand him off his fences rather more and to sit very still in order to give him the time he needed to get his forelegs off the ground. Ridden in this way, Milton could use his rather exaggerated front-leg action to best advantage.

Another problem, and not an unusual one with inexperienced horses, was his inability to shorten his stride. But as he gained confidence in his new rider he learnt to answer such requests from 'on top'. Now, says John, he is so obedient that he responds to aids almost like clockwork. The really great thing about the horse, he says, apart from his outstanding natural athleticism, was his evident love of jumping and his desire to clear every fence.

Towards the end of August the two made their debut together at Leicester Show; just under a fortnight later they appeared again at Rotherham. With Milton's leg injury in mind, John was careful not to do too much with him on the hard ground outdoors. Milton did not qualify for the Horse of the Year Show due to lack of opportunity, so after the Pre-Wembley show at Park Farm he stayed at home to rest while John took Hopscotch and San Salvador south.

When he subsequently set off for the Continent to compete on the World Cup circuit John decided, perhaps somewhat surprisingly in view of the horse's limited competition experience, to take Milton along:

If anything I was short of horses, so I thought I would take him for the experience. It was a matter of trial and error and I didn't expect him to win anything.

For his age he was still very green as far as travelling was concerned. With Caroline he had stayed away from home overnight on only a couple of occasions. But if the countless unfamiliar sights and sounds of big indoor arenas and the hustle and bustle of the often cramped stabling areas came as something of a shock to him, he certainly did not show it.

John's intention was to give him time to settle down and to jump him only in the small classes. But he too – like Caroline and Steve before him – was finding that this horse accomplished everything he was asked to do with almost disdainful ease. 'He coped with the small classes so easily, and was evidently really enjoying himself, that I thought I would put him in something a bit bigger.' In Berlin, in the third week in November, John entered him in the small Grand Prix. He 'lapped it up'and finished a most encouraging third.

The next stop was Brussels a week later. Here again John started by entering him in the small classes but Milton inspired him with such confidence that he felt the time had come to throw his new partner in at the deep end. He put him into the World Cup Qualifier for which the field of 39 included some of the best horses in Europe. Again he coped effortlessly with the step-up in class. He was one of only four to jump double-clear rounds to qualify for the jump-off against the clock. This was

A SEQUENCE SHOWING MILTON JUMPING A BIG TRIPLE BAR. 'THE TAKE-OFF LOOKS A BIT STRANGE,' SAYS JOHN. HE LOOKS AS IF HE MIGHT HAVE SLIPPED, BUT IT'S PROBABLY JUST THAT I'VE PUT HIM IN DEEP. HE TENDS TO GO A BIT TOO HIGH AT TRIPLE BARS AND I HAVE TO GET HIM AS CLOSE AS I CAN, OTHERWISE HE WILL CLIP THE FENCE AS HE COMES DOWN. YOU CAN SEE IN THESE PHOTOS HOW FLEXIBLE HE IS: HE BENDS IN THE MIDDLE. QUITE OFTEN HIS LOWEST POINT OVER A FENCE IS HIS GIRTH

JUMPING THE BIG RUSTIC OXER AT HICKSTEAD

the most difficult task Milton had ever been set and he responded magnificently, jumping another clear round only two seconds slower than April Sun, ridden by Peter Charles, to take second place. In fourth place with a fence down was the horse who was to feature so prominently in Milton's career during the next few years: little Jappeloup, ridden and owned by Pierre Durand.

The last port of call at the beginning of December was Jappeloup's native territory, Bordeaux, where the partisan crowd could always be relied upon to give their home team, and especially their local rider Pierre, maximum support. But John had been so encouraged by Milton's performance in Belgium that he felt he was well up to the challenge of the World Cup Qualifier, with its valuable first-place prize of a Volvo car. Once more Milton jumped a double-clear round, as did seven other horses, from Germany, France, Ireland, Australia and Switzerland. This time, however, despite his inexperience, Milton produced the fastest clear round in the fiercely contested jump-off to record his first major international success and to win his first Volvo. It was a sensational start to his international career and John came home with a pretty shrewd idea that he had a successor to Ryan's Son.

After two such exciting months, the Olympia World Cup in London seemed, on paper at any rate, something of an anti-climax. John, however, was certainly not disheartened. Tiredness after his first trip abroad could have been a factor, and John, like all good riders, is quick to warn against treating horses as machines:

> When a horse has had two good shows people tend to expect him just to carry on winning. But even though Milton had won the World Cup in Bordeaux the week before he was still, up to a point, something of a novice. In fact he didn't go badly at Olympia, he just didn't win very much.

In the World Cup class at the show where Milton was soon to become the star attraction John rode Ryan's Son. Victory went to Jappeloup.

Milton's initiation into the tough world of international jumping had unquestionably been remarkable. When he first joined John Whitaker he had exactly £1,126 in national winnings to his credit. By the end of his short 1985 campaign that total had risen to over £16,000, the bulk of it earned from major Grand Prix events. He had sprung from nowhere to 12th place on the international winnings list for British horses. Milton the super champion was on his way.

CHAPTER 5

A STAR IS BORN

Milton's first complete season as a fully-fledged international horse was a revelation. Right from the start, the quality which perhaps more than any other has kept him at the top of the tree season after season manifested itself virtually overnight: his incredible consistency. It was not simply that he was rarely out of the money, but that rarely did he finish lower than fifth or sixth in high quality jump-off classes. Over the next few years it would become tempting to everyone on the sidelines to forget the adage about horses not being machines and **expect** Milton to get through to every jump-off, or be surprised if he did not jump double clears in Nations Cups.

In the run-up to the last few qualifiers for the 1985-86 World Cup John took him in mid-February to a local indoor show at Rufforth Park where he finished sixth, adding a modest £4.00 to his score sheet. Thereafter he embarked for the bright lights of the big Continental indoor shows: Antwerp, Dortmund, Paris and s'Hertogenbosch. In Antwerp he was placed third in one of the smaller classes and then jumped a double clear in the World Cup Qualifier to go through to the barrage against the clock. He looked set to maintain his Brussels and Bordeaux form of the previous year. What happened next was quite different and is still etched in John's memory: Milton jumped a fence from back to front and was eliminated.

John had seen an opportunity to save time by turning sharply inside one of the fences instead of going round it. It is something, he says, at which Milton is quite good – now. He can land and turn more or less immediately and head for the next obstacle without losing his rhythm. However, at that early stage in their partnership Milton was obviously somewhat confused. John recalls that he got the turn he wanted without any problem but Milton, catching sight of the fence he was supposed to turn inside, totally misunderstood what was wanted. Undaunted by its close proximity and the fact that he was on the landing side, he 'took off from nothing and cleared it by about a foot'. For once his immense scope got him into trouble.

After that, he had a win in Dortmund and finished fourth in the World Cup competition there. He recorded another three clear rounds and was only beaten by the clock in the final jump-off. In the Paris qualifier, won by Jappeloup, he took equal fifth place, and in s'Hertogenbosch he was again fifth in the World Cup as well as equal sixth in a lesser jump-off class. It was a pattern of consistency which would be repeated throughout the season.

After amassing so many World Cup points, which contributed in large measure to John finishing third in the European League, Milton qualified for the final, staged that April in Gothenburg, and John took him to the show along with Hopscotch and San Salvador. But he felt it was too soon for him to tackle a tough championship of that type and he decided to confine him to the lesser competitions. His decision was influenced by an earlier experience with Ryan's Son.

A couple of years before I had jumped Ryan in Gothenburg and at the end the courses were very big. I felt I didn't want to stretch Milton too much at that stage, when he'd still done only half a dozen international shows.

John rode Hopscotch in the final but finished down the field in 25th place. Victory went to the American rider Leslie Burr-Lenehan with the Oldenburg gelding, McLain, who completed the three days with a remarkable zero score. Runners-up,

TRAILING THROUGH THE MUD TO THE PRIZE GIVING AT STOCKHOLM IN 1986 WHERE MILTON FINISHED EITHER FIRST OR SECOND IN EVERY CLASS HE CONTESTED

though at a respectful distance, were Ian Millar and Big Ben, a pair with whom John and Milton would do battle in future finals. It was Big Ben's second appearance in the final, the previous year he had finished eighth.

Returning to England, Milton jumped at Windsor before going to his first Nations Cup show at Hickstead where it came as no surprise to find him nominated to the British team. The Bradleys thought it too soon and would have preferred him to wait, but he duly took his place in the line-up. He made a fairly inauspicious start to his team career, as shown in his first-round total of 12.75 faults. It was to be one of the very rare occasions on which he had Britain's discard score.

MILTON'S GOTHENBURG
DEBUT 1986. HE WOULD
SOON BECOME THE IDOL
OF THE ENTHUSIASTIC
SWEDISH CROWD

Looking back on it John says that far from being a depressing experience it was a highly educative one:

> I learnt a lot that day about how to ride him. I was in a situation where it was important to improve so I really set about thinking why I'd had those fences down. I kept experimenting over the practice fence until I found his best jump. I think my problem was that I was still trying to get him to jump a bit quicker but I found that if I just sat and gave him time, he felt much better. Even though we had got off to a really good start together, you always tend to get a few teething problems with a new horse – little things start to go wrong while you're getting to know each other.

John's assessment of where he had been going wrong in the first round proved correct when Milton produced a much better result in the second half, in which he made only one mistake. John was careful not to bustle him and again collected time faults. Victory went to the French by 24.75 faults to Britain's 30.50. Jappeloup helped the Gallic cause by jumping clear in the second half. Paul Schockemöhle's Deister, still a force to be reckoned with, had the only double clear for the third-placed German team.

After this 'getting to know you' experience the British public had a much more accurate picture of things to come at the Royal International ten days later, when John went through the card like a bullet: with Ryan's Son he won the King George V Gold Cup; with San Salvador he won four classes, including the 'Jump and Drive' for which the prize was a Maestro car. And with Milton he won the Everest Double Glazing Grand Prix, the horse's first major triumph on home soil, as well as finishing third in the *Daily Mail* Cup. One of San Salvador's victories was in the Hedex Speed Stakes – if anyone needed headache tablets, it was John's rivals. As the year progressed they would find themselves needing them more and more as the grey gelding began, inexorably, to show his true mettle.

Milton continued on his impressive way, gaining good placings in both Germany and France and winning the Derby in Dinard during August. On his only other appearance in a Derby, at Falsterbo the following summer, he finished third, again proving himself most adept at this type of marathon event with its permanent cross-country type obstacles. However, John understands Doreen and Tom Bradley's fears about the Derby at Hickstead. There the steep 10ft 6in descent from the big bank is more difficult that anything on the French or Swedish courses. 'Milton is quite sensible,' he says, and he doubts that he would try to jump off the top, as some horses have done. But he knows all too well from personal experience that there is still an element of risk.

Hopscotch hurt himself quite badly at the Hickstead bank in 1991. He stumbled on the way down, crumpled on to his knees at the bottom and in so doing must have struck into himself. John managed to stay in the saddle, Hopscotch scrambled up again and they carried on. It was not until the horse was on his way back to the stables that it was noticed he had taken a big piece out of his leg. 'He was never lame, but the cut only just missed his tendon sheath.' It was a close shave and John feels he would rather not have the responsibility of Milton's owners saying 'We'll leave it up to you' and then have something similar happen to his top horse.

Shortly after Dinard, Milton made his second Nations Cup appearance, in Rotterdam. The strong British team, Nick Skelton on Airborne, Michael Whitaker with his Olympic mare Amanda, Janet Hunter on Lisnamarrow, and John with Milton, swept all before them to defeat the Swiss by a margin of nearly two fences. Only two horses from the ten teams recorded double clears, the redoubtable Deister and the future German Olympic team gold medallist, The Freak, ridden at that time by Austria's Hugo Simon. Milton put up the next best performance, clearing all the fences and collecting just a quarter of a time fault in the first round, and half in the second. It was the best performance by a British horse and set the style for the grey's future Nations Cup appearances.

After Rotterdam, John took him to Stockholm where he enjoyed a tremendous week. He won one big class and finished second in three others, including the Grand Prix, won by The Freak. Then came the greatest moment of his career to date: he went with the British team to Calgary in Canada. The journey to this far-flung spot on the CSIO circuit may be long and arduous but everyone who has ever been there agrees that it is worth it. Ron and Marg Southern's magnificent Spruce Meadows is one of the most resplendent show grounds in the show jumping world. Everyone is treated as a VIP and the level of prize money is as breathtaking as the scenery.

MILTON MADE HIS AACHEN DEBUT IN 1986, THOUGH NOT IN THE WORLD CHAMPIONSHIPS. AT THAT TIME HIS MANE WAS PLAITED FOR COMPETITIONS, BUT LATER JOHN DECIDED TO LEAVE IT LOOSE BECAUSE THE PLAITS IRRITATED MILTON WHILE HE WAS JUMPING

The Nations Cup may not attract as many teams as most of its European counterparts but it is always a hotly contested affair, with top riders from the United States trying to outdo the cream of the Canadian squad and fend off the challenge from across the Atlantic. This time Canada was fielding its new World Champion, Gail Greenough on Mr T, as well as World Cup runner-up Ian Millar with Big Ben. But not even they could keep up with the Americans and the British, who forged ahead in the first round and finished the second in equal first place on four faults – two fences ahead of the host nation.

The jump-off against the clock was one of the closest fought in the history of Nations Cups, the Americans Robert Ridland, Jennifer Newell, Joan Scharffenberger and Hap Hansen recording eight faults, four and two clear rounds, respectively. The British quartet, Michael Whitaker, Nick Skelton, Malcolm Pyrah and John, responded in like fashion. But Hap Hansen's round on Juniperus was substantially faster than the others and it proved decisive when each team's times were totalled. Victory went to the USA by the incredibly narrow margin of nine-hundredths of a second. Apart from Joan Scharffenberger's partner Winnipeg, Milton was the only horse to jump three clear rounds.

He underlined his claim to be the most exciting newcomer on the international scene on the final day of the show in the du Maurier International, the world's richest Grand Prix. Overall prize-money that year stood at £90,000. Only four horses jumped double-clear rounds, Milton, Lavendal, ridden for Canada by Laura Tidball-Balisky, Puschkin for Switzerland (Markus Fuchs) and Jappeloup for France. It was Milton's biggest test to date and he addressed it in immaculate fashion, jumping one of only two clear rounds against the clock in a time that was nearly seven seconds faster than Lavendal's. He came away with a first prize of over £28,000.

If he found any difficulty in switching from an outdoor show to the confined Wembley arena for his first Horse of the Year Show, he certainly showed no sign of it. He recorded four good placings from his four starts. In the Leading Jumper of the Year on the Wednesday he finished third behind Sue Pountain on Ned Kelly VI, and David Broome on Phoenix Park, beaten by little more than half a second. With a slightly better position from the draw – he was fourth in the nine-horse jump-off – and had he not slipped as John turned him to the fourth fence from home, he might well have won. On the closing night he produced the fastest round in the jump-off for the Everest Double Glazing Grand Prix but a fence down put him second behind Malcolm Pyrah and Towerlands Anglezarke.

Thereafter he was consistently in the money at the Brussels, Bordeaux and Olympia World Cup, finishing runner-up in the Grand Prix at the latter, once again to Anglezarke.

When the prize-money figures for the year were announced the writing was clearly on the wall for the rest of Britain's riders and owners. Milton had taken over the crown vacated by the leader of the previous two years, St James, who went into retirement at the close of that season. Milton's total of £71,617 was more than £20,000 in excess of that achieved by runner-up Anglezarke. For a horse in his first full international season it was a tremendous achievement. It was only the beginning.

CHAPTER 6

THE OPPOSITION

No assessment of Milton's achievements would be complete without an evaluation of the opposition: fame and fortune were not due to his being the only bright star in a dimly lit firmament. Indeed, it is due to his two greatest assets – extraordinary jumping ability coupled with quite remarkable consistency – that he has enjoyed such a glittering career at a time when show jumping world wide has definitely not been short of brilliant horses.

In addition to Milton, the second half of the 1980s threw up a fair number of remarkable jumpers, of whom two at least could be called outstanding. One, the near-black French horse called Jappeloup, began to make his name internationally in 1982, while Milton was still at the novice stage, and then for five seasons was a regular rival of the grey. The other, the year-younger Big Ben, competes for Canada and so has been a less frequent adversary on the European circuit, though he and Milton have several times matched strides at championship level, they are as different as chalk from cheese in appearance. All three horses have provided some tremendous sport for show jumping fans, though for Doreen Bradley it was always competition from the French horse she feared most during the years that his and Milton's careers overlapped.

Jappeloup, named after the area where he was born, was foaled two years before Milton in April 1975. Sired by a trotter, Tyrol II, out of a thoroughbred mare called Vénérable, he was a *Selle Français* [French Riding Horse], though to look at he was certainly not typical of a French competition horse. To begin with he was very small – only a fraction over 15.2hh – and he had a natural tendency to be rather clumsy, the sort of animal who is always stepping on people's feet. He also lacked the well-coordinated paces of a quality French Riding Horse and was a far from comfortable ride. The main reason for this was that his back end was taller than his front – meaning he stood 'croup high'. This type of conformation is frequently found in trotting horses and Jappeloup evidently inherited it through his sire. For show jumping purposes it is not ideal, since it tends to make a horse carry too much weight on his forehand, making it difficult for him to get his legs and shoulders off the ground on take-off. It was a problem in his early days, one which had to be remedied by concentrated work on the flat and by gymnastic work over small fences.

When Pierre Durand, by profession a lawyer specialising in bankruptcy, but a keen amateur show jumper at weekends, first had the chance to buy him when the horse was rising four, he turned him down because of his diminutive size. However, as with John Whitaker and Milton, fate interceded. The following year Pierre was again asked to try the little horse and this time, impressed by his explosive way of jumping fences, he decided to overlook his shortcomings and buy him. Jappeloup was duly installed in Pierre's modest stables, situated at one end of a small equestrian centre at St-Seurin-sur-l'Isle, near St Emilion.

The gelding, a self-contained little character, brave, careful and bouncing with energy, turned out, like Milton, to be an extremely spooky individual. In Jappeloup's case this spookiness could well have jeopardised his jumping career. In the early part of his partnership with Pierre, he had a habit of jamming on his brakes with lightning speed at a fence he did not like the look of. He had a particular aversion to narrow, dark coloured obstacles. With nothing much in front of him, because of the horse's small stature, Pierre could not always avoid making an unscheduled exit. On these

JAPPELOUP IN ACTION IN ROTTERDAM, 1989, WHEN HE LOST HIS EUROPEAN TITLE TO MILTON

occasions Jappeloup would often slip his head from his bridle and go for a gallop round the arena. Just such a débacle occurred during their first Olympic appearance.

After this experience Pierre devoted much time to improving the horse's technique, to understanding the character of his athletic but unpredictable little partner and to advancing his own skills as a rider. The Frenchman was sometimes criticised for cracking under pressure and the fact that he rode much less than international rivals such as John Whitaker certainly put him at a disadvantage. This was particularly evident in the 1986 World Championships at Aachen. By this time he and Jappeloup had really got their act together and the gelding emerged from the three tough legs of the championships as the top horse, the only one from 72 starters not to have a fence down. It qualified Pierre, along with Canada's Gail Greenough,

Britain's Nick Skelton and Conrad Homfeld from the United States for the 'change-horse' individual final.

In this event each of the four riders jumps his own horse as well as the horse of each of the other finalists over an identical course, built on rather more modest lines than normal international courses. It has long been a controversial event, since it is more a test of the rider than of a horse/rider partnership and even then luck and the order in which riders draw the horses play a significant part. On this occasion Nick Skelton found himself riding Gail's horse, Mr T, immediately after Pierre, who had not got on too well with him. Mr T (who, as mentioned, was in Caroline's yard at the same time as Milton) was in a nervous state when Nick climbed aboard and was, he said, running away going to the first fence. He subsequently had a stop and time faults at the combination and although Nick had clear rounds on the three other horses he came away with only a bronze medal.

The person who came away with no medal at all was, predictably, Pierre. Afterwards he admitted to being a little disappointed that he had nothing to show for being a finalist in a competition where a title was at stake. But he had recognised beforehand that he was at a disadvantage because he was an amateur whose competition work was virtually restricted to weekends. He had, he said, ridden only about 20 horses altogether in competition during his entire career. But he had enjoyed seeing Jappeloup in the hands of such good riders and was particularly gratified at the obvious high esteem in which the others held his horse.

Gail Greenough, who completed the final without faults, said that if she could keep one of the other riders' horses, she would have chosen Jappeloup: 'When he jumps you really have to hold on.' Nick agreed: the horse he enjoyed riding most was Jappeloup and he would not have minded in the least taking him home.

Unlike any other show jumping championship though, the World title is primarily won by the rider and it is difficult to think in terms of any of the horses in the final as failing. Most riders consider it an unsatisfactory conclusion to a World Championship. In the past some even objected to it on the grounds that it could be detrimental and confusing to their horses to be ridden suddenly by someone different. Nowadays that criticism is not often heard and when, four years later, Milton qualified for the change-horse final at the World Equestrian Games neither John Whitaker nor the Bradleys were concerned that it would do him any harm.

It was, incidentally, during Aachen 1986, while Pierre and Jappeloup were striving for a world title, that Milton quietly made his debut on the famous German show ground. For the championships John had opted to ride the more experienced horse, Hopscotch, his partner from the previous year's Europeans. He admits that he was tempted to put Milton in instead but says that he had really made up his mind not to before he set off for Aachen. However, Milton was John's other entry for the show and he gave him two outings in non-championship classes, once each on the first and second days of the show. He finished third on day one and second on day two, without touching a fence.

Later that year Milton would be back to jumping on level terms with Jappeloup and thereafter following very much in the little spring-heeled horse's hoofprints. In the first six seasons of his ten-year career, Jappeloup would jump ten double-clear rounds in Nations Cups. So would Milton (but for time faults, Milton's score would have been 12). Jappeloup would become European Champion. So would Milton. Jappeloup had qualified for the individual final of the World Championships. So too would Milton. No wonder Doreen Bradley considered him the chief danger to her beloved grey, but, she said, 'Jappeloup wasn't the same Jappeloup after the Seoul Olympics.' And many would agree with her.

The little horse's 1987 season was phenomenal: Nations Cup successes in Rome and Aachen, where he jumped double clears, Grand Prix victories in La Baule, Amsterdam, Vienna and Brussels and double gold medals in the European Championships in St Gallen.

Runner-up to Big Ben in the World Cup final the following spring, and again in the winning team at Aachen, the French horse competed with a judicious mixture

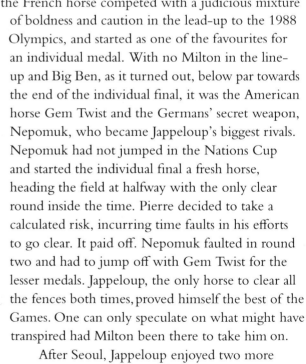

of boldness and caution in the lead-up to the 1988 Olympics, and started as one of the favourites for an individual medal. With no Milton in the line-up and Big Ben, as it turned out, below par towards the end of the individual final, it was the American horse Gem Twist and the Germans' secret weapon, Nepomuk, who became Jappeloup's biggest rivals. Nepomuk had not jumped in the Nations Cup and started the individual final a fresh horse, heading the field at halfway with the only clear round inside the time. Pierre decided to take a calculated risk, incurring time faults in his efforts to go clear. It paid off. Nepomuk faulted in round two and had to jump off with Gem Twist for the lesser medals. Jappeloup, the only horse to clear all the fences both times, proved himself the best of the Games. One can only speculate on what might have transpired had Milton been there to take him on.

After Seoul, Jappeloup enjoyed two more pretty successful seasons without quite recapturing his pre-Games brilliance. Advancing years and perhaps to a certain extent his exertions in Korea, began to take their toll. In 1991, when he was 16,

AFTER WINNING THE GRAND PRIX BIG BEN SURVEYS THE SHOW GROUND AT CALGARY 1991. STANDING 17.3HH HE PROBABLY HAS A SUPERB VIEW

Pierre restricted his appearances to a few selected Grand Prix competitions – a sort of farewell tour of those shows where he had enjoyed his biggest triumphs. He was retired at the Paris Masters show in September that year. One morning a few weeks later he was found dead in his box. The big heart which had carried that little body to so many triumphs had seen him through to the end of his competing days and then simply given out.

The aptly named Big Ben (originally known as Winston) was foaled a year before Milton in 1976. By the French stallion Etretat, he was born in Belgium and acquired by Ian Millar in 1983 at the instigation of Dutch dealer Emile Hendrix. While on a visit to Holland, Ian took Emile's advice to go and view what he described as 'a very interesting horse' in international rider Bert Romp's yard. As soon as Ian set eyes on the giant chestnut gelding – who at 17.3hh stands a full five inches taller than Milton and more than eight inches taller than Jappeloup – he liked the look of him. He liked him even more when Bert Romp began to put him through his paces and then, climbing into the saddle himself, found him equally good to ride. It took the Canadian less than half-an-hour to decide that he wanted this handsome gelding.

With the help of an old friend Ian managed to find the purchase price and together they formed a syndicate called Canadian Show Jumpers Unlimited Inc which has owned the horse ever since. Ian and his wife Lynn hold a handful of the 40 shares and the rest are divided between numerous shareholders. They follow Big Ben's career with close interest. In fact at major events the gelding probably has more people cheering him on from the owners' stand than almost all of the other horses put together.

Big Ben arrived in Canada in the autumn of 1983, at the very time when Milton's life was also undergoing radical change. Initially the big gelding's progress was fairly slow. Ian found that, just like Jappeloup, he had a tendency to spook at unfamiliar fences and this had to be overcome through patient and repetitive schooling. Also, and unusually for a gelding, Ben is a rather aggressive character and with such horses it is especially important to avoid confrontations. A horse who constantly fights his rider is never going to go far in top level competition. In the stable, again like Jappeloup, he can be aloof, happily taking his favourite titbit, a carrot, from his groom or Ian's wife, but turning them down from strangers. And, says Ian, he can spot a vet at two hundred paces. Big Ben and Milton evidently have more than jumping ability in common.

Ian knew that Ben's many strengths far outweighed his minor weaknesses: he possesses abundant natural jumping ability, he is a remarkably fast learner and he is exceptionally well put together for such a big horse. As a result he is well balanced and can use his great strength to maximum effect. Size does not necessarily have any bearing on how high or wide a horse can jump, as little Jappeloup, to name but one, has amply proved, but big international courses do tend to take more out of the smaller individual than the bigger, more robust type.

Provided he has the necessary natural spring and has been trained to carry himself and his rider in balance, the problem of clearing the actual individual fences is much the same for any horse. What makes the difference between success or failure over, say, a 12 or 13 fence course, which includes at least one double and one treble combination, is the horse's ability to lengthen and shorten his stride instantly when requested by the rider. Only if he can do this accurately and without losing his balance will he be able to cope with the distances in combinations, and between obstacles set at related distances to each other, and successfully jump the obstacles as well. After all, it is the rider, not the horse, who has walked the course, measured everything out and based his strategy on his particular horse's strengths and weaknesses. The horse must therefore be trained to put his trust in his rider and respond to requests for a lengthened or shortened stride if he is successfully to negotiate a technically demanding course.

Big Ben has been endowed by nature with an enormous stride in keeping with his enormous physique and to begin with, like Milton when John first rode him, he did not appreciate that he must learn to shorten it on demand. However, once he had mastered this essential skill, he found jumping at Grand Prix level a piece of cake. And of course he has the added advantage in a jump-off against the clock of being able to eat up the ground between fences with his great raking stride. Ben has often been seen to win a class on time without appearing to hurry at all − it is just that he can, when required, cover more ground with each stride than his smaller rivals.

Ian, now in his third decade of world-class jumping, has no hesitation in nominating Big Ben 'the best horse I have ever had the pleasure of riding.' Their major successes together have included numerous Grand Prix and Nations Cup competitions, the silver medal in the 1986 World Cup, team and individual gold the following year in the Pan American Games, victory in the 1988 World Cup and a repeat success in this indoor championship twelve months later, when they held off a spirited challenge from John and Milton who eventually finished runners-up. This 1989 victory made Ian only the second rider to win the World Cup twice and the first to take it in successive years. Big Ben was the first horse to win two Cups and also made history by winning all three legs of the final, an achievement which even Milton has not equalled. At the time of writing that record still stands.

Ian says of his giant partner, for whom 1992 was his ninth year at Grand Prix level,

Some horses get very sour if they're on the road a lot, but Ben's the absolute exact opposite of that. He is not a stay-at-home type. He gets bored very fast when he's at home. He'll relax for a week at most, then he wants to go and do something. When the truck leaves without him he gets in quite a state. We have even taken him to quite a few shows where he hasn't been competing, just so that I can keep riding him and working him. He really enjoys that. Also, given his size and his strength, jumping these big fences does not exact the same toll that it does from some horses. He's such a strong horse that I'd say he probably expends less energy doing the job than a lot of his rivals.

One occasion, however, when even Big Ben finished a tired horse, was at the Seoul Olympics in 1988. Ian, competing in his fourth Games, must have felt that at last he was due for a medal. His previous best chance had been in 1980 but Canada, in common with the majority of top equestrian nations, decided to boycot the Moscow Olympiad. At the International Show Jumping Festival, staged in Rotterdam by the FEI as compensation for all these countries, the Canadians, including Ian on Brother Sam, scored a famous victory over the British. Ian came away with a gold medal, but as team and individual runner-up John Whitaker said wistfully of his own two silvers, achieved on Ryan's Son, 'It's just a pity they aren't the real thing.'

Four years later in Los Angeles John did achieve the real thing in the team championship, again with Ryan's Son. And it was there that Big Ben, like Jappeloup, made his Olympic debut. However, since he had been with Ian for less than a year and was still a relatively inexperienced eight-year-old, it came as no surprise that he did not feature among the medals – though the team did come tantalisingly close to taking the bronze, finishing less than one fault behind the West Germans. In the individual standings Big Ben finished equal 14th alongside, significantly, Jappeloup and Ryan's Son.

Seoul looked like being a very different matter. By that time Big Ben had proved himself one of the world's top horses and, in the absence of Milton, he and Jappeloup seemed set to dominate the shake-up for the individual medals. After jumping a clear round in the second half of the team championship, in which Canada again narrowly missed a medal, Ian looked to be well in contention for the individual final on the last day of the Games. But, as he admitted later, he simply 'ran out of horse'. Afterwards the articulate Canadian, with his typically intellectual approach, tried to analyse just what had gone wrong but came to no positive conclusions. Perhaps the horse's energy had after all been sapped by the World Cup victory, or by the extensive Canadian qualifying system for the Olympics, or simply the long journey to Korea. 'Post Olympics we were never able to put our finger on why he didn't go better in Seoul,' Ian said after his second World Cup win the following year. 'There was no apparent reason – but we were definitely dealing with a tired horse in Seoul.' One thing Ian and many of his rivals were critical of was the formula for the show jumping championships in Seoul.

The final part of the individual event was actually the sixth of seven rounds at those Olympics. I hope we won't see that formula again because it turned the whole thing into an endurance contest and was far more jumping than these horses would normally do in a few days.

The formula was indeed changed, and the amount of competitions reduced, for the 1992 Games.

Big Ben, unlike Milton, has had to overcome some fairly serious health problems since making his international debut. Something which occurred in April 1988 might well have been an advance warning. After winning the World Cup Final in Gothenburg Ian Millar revealed that the horse had been a little unwell before the final leg and that colic had been suspected. When the time came to jump he was fit enough and finished a good third, which was sufficient to give him overall victory over Jappeloup. But after he had been flown back to the United States he was found to be running a temperature and was grounded for two weeks before he could return home to Canada. He was then, as we have seen, not his brilliant best at the Olympic Games.

Then early in 1990 he did actually succumb to a bout of colic and had to undergo surgery. It deprived him of a chance to go for a third World Cup Final. He was again laid low with colic 12 months later, and again forced to miss the World Cup. Remarkably, he fought his way back to fitness and between June and November 1991, at the age of 15, his successes on the World Cup circuit alone included victory in the Calgary qualifier, three second places and three thirds. Notwithstanding these setbacks, Big Ben has proved himself one of the best show jumpers of his day and a worthy adversary for Milton and Jappeloup.

Apart from these two outstanding championship horses, Milton has over the years regularly faced opposition from a galaxy of other top-class Grand Prix horses. When Milton first appeared on the international scene Paul Schockemöhle's remarkable three-times European Champion Deister was still competing, though the two horses' careers did not really overlap to a significant degree. More recently there have been the same owner's impressive chestnut Hannoverian, Walzerkönig, ridden by Franke Sloothaak; the French stallion, Quito de Baussy (Eric Navet), and his fleet-footed compatriot, Norton de Rhuys (Roger-Yves Bost); some particularly good Dutch and Belgian-bred horses such as the Dutch Warmblood, Felix, who was ridden by Jos Lansink before being sold to Japan, and the Belgian-bred, Egano, also the mount of Lansink. There was also the German-bred mare, Dollar Girl, ridden to many victories by Switzerland's Thomas Fuchs before her owner decided to remove her from Fuchs' stables and transfer her, ironically enough, first to John Whitaker's stables in early 1992 and later to Nick Skelton's. And, though less frequently, Milton has met up with the cream of the American side, notably his look-alike, Gem Twist.

Gem Twist's performance in Seoul was particularly noteworthy. His rider, Greg Best, had only started competing at Grand Prix level in February 1987. Six months

before the Games he still had no inkling that before the end of the year he would be competing at the Oympics, let alone winning a medal. Then he won the first American selection trial and before he knew what had happened, he had booked a ticket to Seoul. Two years later Gem Twist, bred and owned by former top American rider turned trainer Frank Chapot, qualified for the individual final at the World Equestrian Games. Gem Twist's style of jumping is rather different from Milton's: he is a sharper horse altogether and, says Greg, likes to do things his way. The overall impression is that he runs on at his fences, but can, when necessary, get himself out of trouble, whereas Milton approaches his calmly and in complete accord with John.

Walzerkönig, two years Milton's junior, has enjoyed tremendous success in the hands of Franke Sloothaak, one of the most skilful and accurate riders in the world. Together they won a team gold medal in Seoul, finished third in the 1990 World Cup Final and took the individual silver in the European Championships of 1991. Unlike Milton and Gem Twist, Walzerkönig is no oil painting to look at. But handsome is as handsome does and his tremendous scope, coupled with the ability to turn on a sixpence, makes him a particularly dangerous rival in any jump-off against the clock.

The French Stallion, Quito de Baussy, who like Marius combines stud duties with a jumping career, burst onto the scene in Stockholm where he took over the crown vacated by Mr T. He confirmed that his victory was no fluke by deposing Milton at the European Championships 12 months later. He is certainly not an easy horse to ride in a speed class or in a jump-off because of his tendency to buck and kick when his rider tries to push him on, but he has a habit of jumping clear rounds over big Grand Prix tracks just when it matters most and in Eric Navet he has a most sympathetic partner.

These are just some of the top horses and riders Milton has come up against. Their achievements speak for themselves and prove that Milton's success has been no walkover. His adoring fans would no doubt like him to be invincible and it has been tempting at times to think of him that way and to be dismayed when he (or for that matter John) has proved fallible; but no show jumper, including the brilliant ones mentioned here, is unbeatable.

Horses who are *nearly* unbeatable do occur in one or two areas of equestrianism. An outstanding dressage horse can dominate the sport for many seasons, a contributory factor being that the set test remains virtually the same competition after competition and the rider can concentrate on polishing the various movements of this one performance. In different circumstances a 'wonder horse' like Arkle comes along, possessed of a freak extra gear, and barring a fall no one can beat him on the racecourse except the handicapper.

But show jumping is another matter entirely. There never has been and probably never will be an 'unbeatable' horse. To begin with each course is totally different from the last and, with the rare exception of Derbies, never jumped again, so the horse is faced with an entirely new set of problems every time he competes which, of course, he does far more often than the average dressage horse or steeplechaser. By the law of averages, he has many more chances of making a mistake.

Then there is the fact that the rider has only a brief time to study the fences for each competition and to work out how best to answer the questions posed by the course designer. Modern show jumping is not just about being able to clear big heights and spreads. Technical problems are increasingly used to separate those at the top of the tree. It therefore follows that a lack of communication, a slight misjudgement or a last-minute change of mind on the rider's part can spell disaster no matter how talented the horse. Not even the most athletic animal can get out of trouble in which he has been landed by his human partner. As Mrs Bradley says, if the rider does not tell the horse what type of fence it is, how does he know? Certainly miscalculation of time can never be blamed on the horse, for it is the clock in the rider's head which governs how fast or slow the pair go.

Another consideration is the draw, which in this sport can have tremendous influence on the ultimate result of a class. Competitors drawn late are, as a general rule, at a considerable advantage because they have time to sit at the ringside and watch their rivals. This gives them the opportunity to see whether the course is riding as they expected or whether unseen problems are emerging. In a competition judged on speed, they can assess where best to risk a tight turn to save precious seconds or, if a gamble they were planning to take is proved by other riders to be too difficult, they can switch to an alternative plan. The draw, particularly in a jump-off, often makes the difference between success and failure. Even Milton, despite jumping immaculate clear rounds, has lost more than one important class because of an early draw in a big jump-off when a later competitor has been able to beat his time.

Some brilliant horses fail to achieve their full potential because they never meet up with the right rider. In this respect Milton has been twice blessed. Deprived of Caroline's support at a crucial time in his career, he was fortunate to be teamed with John Whitaker. The same can be said of their closest rivals, wonderful horses matched with their ideal human partners.

Add all these factors together, take into account the numerous other brilliant horses and riders there are in the world, then look at Milton's career record and it helps to explain why so many people, Britain's long-time team manager Ronnie Massarella among them, consider him the greatest show jumper the world has seen. His scope, his consistency, his technical prowess, his whole attitude to competition, not to mention his sheer presence: these are his supreme qualities.

READY FOR TAKE-OFF:
ONE EAR LISTENS TO HIS
RIDER AS MILTON SIZES UP
THE FENCE AHEAD

CHAPTER 7

CHAMPIONSHIP DEBUT

Milton's 1987 seasonal warm-up again took place at Rufforth Park in February. As in the previous year he finished sixth. This time the prize-money had risen to £5.00. A few days later he set off for Belgium, Germany and Sweden. He was second in three consecutive World Cup Qualifiers, in Antwerp, Dortmund and Gothenburg, won the Grand Prix at the latter and came away from the three shows with £17,500 to his credit. In the Antwerp Qualifier he jumped three clear rounds and was beaten by Harvey Smith on Sanyo Shining Example, by a little over half a second. In Dortmund he jumped another three clears and was a mere one-third of a second adrift of the winner, Hugo Simon on Winzer. In Gothenburg he jumped two clears but finally had a fence down in the jump-off against the clock behind the German rider Michael Rüping on Silbersee.

John finished runner-up in the European League with 70 points, just 12 behind the winner, Paul Schockemöhle. Of those 70, Milton had contributed all but six. John considered that the horse was ready to make his championship debut. Accordingly he took him to Paris in the second week of April for his first Volvo World Cup Final.

The show started, or to be more accurate did **not** start, in chaotic circumstances. It was the first time that Paris had hosted the final in the nine-year history of this great winter indoor championship; expectations were high that the French would make a superb job of it. The venue, the ultra modern Palais Omnisports arena at Bercy, seemed well nigh perfect. Yet, inconceivably, the show came close to suffering the same fate as the concurrent Badminton Horse Trials in Britain, which had to be called off at the last moment because of wet weather.

Most members of the British equestrian press had been sent by their respective journals to cover Badminton. Only a couple had headed for the alternative show jumping attraction. When the former found themselves suddenly re-routed to Paris it was in the confident expectation of joining their smug, dry colleagues for a trouble-free few days under cover. 'The benefits of an indoor venue during the month of April,' wrote the correspondent for *The Independent*, with understandable confidence, 'will be appreciated by the six British show jumping riders who have qualified for this year's World Cup final. Rain has not been able to threaten their big date in Paris . . .' Their astonishment at finding, upon arrival, the world's top show jumpers threatening to stage a walk-out because of the waterlogged state of the ground knew no bounds.

One could but wonder at the wisdom of holding stock-car racing on the same ground that was to be used 15 days later for an equestrian event, but that is what had happened at the Palais Omnisports. It should have come as no surprise to anyone that such goings on would leave fragments of metal and glass in their wake. With just a fortnight to go before one of the biggest and most prestigious horse shows of the year, the organising committee, under its president Jacinte Giscard d'Estaing, found itself with a totally useless ground. Rather than attempt to extract the debris, they had wisely decided to have the entire covering removed from the arena and to replace it with a similar load from the same source. Fine in theory, disastrous, as it turned out, in practice. The new earth was delivered in good time. But it had to be stored outside for a couple of days before it could be laid in the arena and no one thought to give it any protection. And the inevitable happened: the same wet weather which had pulverised the Duke of Beaufort's park at Badminton took itself to Paris, reducing the new ground material to the consistency of clay.

When the cream of the world's riders, 43 of them from 11 countries and four continents, arrived at the arena the majority took one look at the ground and refused point blank to risk their horses. The British, John Whitaker among them, declared it much too dangerous. The American, Conrad Homfeld, at that time the only rider to have won two World Cups (in 1980 on Balbuco and 1985 on Abdullah), summed it up when he said that he was by no means unhappy not to be competing that year. Still on crutches after breaking his femur in a fall a few weeks previously, he said he was positively glad not to be faced with the terrible decision of whether or not to jump: 'You wouldn't want to risk *any* horse on this going.' Frenchman Hubert Bourdy was prevailed upon to test the conditions with a non-World Cup horse and proclaimed it 'impossible'.

The show had no alternative but to cancel the warm-up competitions scheduled for the Wednesday, which was hard luck on the thousands of school children who had been given free tickets, courtesy of the French Post Office. A last-minute salvage operation began. Finally, and not, in the opinion of a good many people, before time, it was discovered that the cooling system for the ice rink in the arena could be reversed and used to heat the earth from below. This, together with the addition of chalk and a topping of sawdust, produced by the following day an acceptable jumping surface.

Substitute preliminary classes were hastily scheduled to give the riders a chance to warm up their horses. John Whitaker got off to a good start by winning the first, though not with Milton but on his speed horse San Salvador. He took the grey at a more leisurely pace and jumped a clear round just outside the time to finish in 26th place, one below Canada's Ian Millar and Big Ben. Later that day the first stage of Milton's first World Cup Final went ahead.

This opening competition has always been the trickiest of the three. It is a Table C class, one round against the clock. Several seconds are added for each fence down and the fastest total time wins. Normally a Grand Prix horse like Milton would not be entered for such an event, but the object of including it in a championship is to test every facet of each horse and rider. Milton finished a disappointing 16th but John said it was as much his fault as the horse's. Because it is a speed class, he says, there is a tendency to try to go too fast even though the fences are quite big (the rules stipulate 'Table C over a big Table A course'). 'You might get one or two fliers but usually if you jump a safe round and try to get in the first five you are still in with a chance of winning the whole thing. That year I tried to go too fast. I had one fence down and then instead of keeping the same rhythm I tried to go quicker to make up for it and had another.'

Milton's first mistake came at a big oxer in the middle of the treble at the eighth. He was one of more than a dozen horses to be in trouble at this combination. Thereafter he looked like being clear until John decided to ask him to stand off the 12th and last fence. It was too big a task even for Milton and he took the top rail off. Aware that he had misjudged things, John said he was more disappointed in himself than in Milton. However, the second leg, a Table A with two jump-offs, the second against the clock, went much better. Milton, relishing the bigger fences, faulted just once in the first round which was good enough to give him equal seventh place and pull him up to 13th after the first two legs.

Scoring in the final is a somewhat complicated process which works as follows: points are given to all competitors who finish the initial round of the first two legs. The winner in both competitions gets one point more than the number of starters in the first leg; the second has two points less than the winner; the third three points less than the winner and so on. After the first two legs each rider's points for the two classes are totalled and converted into faults. The two-day leader is given a zero score. The penalties of the others are calculated by multiplying with the coefficient of 0.50 the difference between their number of World Cup points and the points of the leading competitor after two competitions.

In practice what this boils down to is that it is imperative for a rider to go well in the opening speed leg if he is to have any chance of winning the overall championship. He can jump three clear rounds on day two and another two on day three, but if the winner of the speed competition goes equally well, there is no way in which he can be overtaken – other than by being beaten by the clock in the second-leg jump-off or by collecting a lot of time faults in the third leg. Indeed it is perfectly feasible for a horse who has not hit a fence throughout the contest to lose out to one who has a fence down on day one but records a faster time.

Riders have levelled criticism at this format over the years because it tends to put too much emphasis on the speed competition but no one has been able to come up with a better idea. Even though it took John a few years to judge the first leg correctly, he feels that when all is said and done it is right to have a speed class followed by a jump-off competition since it demonstrates the horses' versatility. Additionally, because of the way the points conversion system works there is invariably less than the cost of a fence separating the leading riders after the first two days. With the horses required to jump in reverse order of merit on day three, this has always produced a tremendously

HICKSTEAD 1987.
MILTON SCORED A TWO-
ROUND TOTAL OF FOUR
FAULTS IN THE NATIONS
CUP, THOUGH THE
BRITISH TEAM COULD
ONLY FINISH FIFTH

gripping spectacle for the crowd.

The 1987 final was a perfect example of the nail-biting entertainment provided by such a format. The leader going into the last leg, two rounds over a Grand Prix course, was the American Katharine Burdsall on The Natural, a horse who always created a great deal of interest because he changed hands not so long before for one million dollars. The Natural had won the first leg with the fastest clear round and finished runner-up to Frenchman Philippe Rozier on Malesan Jiva in the second. Austria's Hugo Simon, at that time the only European rider ever to have won the World Cup (the inaugural running in Gothenburg in 1979 with the great Gladstone), had finished third in both legs on his new partner, the grey Winzer. All three of these horses had jumped triple-clear rounds on day two, with less than a second dividing them in the timed jump-off. Hugo, with a two-day total of two faults, and Philippe, on 3.50, were close enough to the leader to cash in on any mistakes.

By the halfway stage on day three The Natural had relinquished the lead to the attractive bay Anglo-Arab Jiva, much to the delight of the 12,000-strong Parisian crowd. Not quite so foot perfect this time, The Natural bounced one pole so high out of its cups that it seemed incredible that it did not fall. He got away with that mistake but not with another misjudgement at the penultimate fence, a big vertical of rails and planks. With time penalties to add as well, he finished with a score of 4.50, 1.00 behind Jiva who had jumped a copybook clear.

However, The Natural came back with a fine faultless effort on his second appearance, putting pressure on Jiva to do likewise if Europe was to regain the Cup from the North Americans. Sadly the host nation's hopes were dashed when Jiva faulted at the first element of the treble combination. This proved a testing line of fences, a vertical Liverpool (rails over a water ditch) to an oxer to an oxer/Liverpool, set by course designer Philippe Gayot. Anxious to have enough pace to tackle the second and third elements, Philippe Rozier approached the first a shade too fast and paid the penalty. So The Natural took the Cup back across the Atlantic, Philippe was runner-up, beaten by three faults, and Katharine Birdsall's compatriot Lisa Jacquin with the Thoroughbred ex-racehorse, For the Moment, came up to take the bronze medal.

Yet despite the overall outcome it was Milton who was the undoubted star of that final leg. As he was to prove over and over again in the future, the bigger the tracks became the more they suited him. Together with Jiva, Paul Schockemöhle's Deister, Big Ben and Jappeloup, he was faultless over the testing 12-fence track in the first round. Then over the slightly shortened second-round course he again went brilliantly, to finish with the only double clear of the day. It pulled him right up into equal fifth place overall with Big Ben. One can only speculate on what might have been had he finished higher up the scoreboard in the first leg. Not surprisingly, John was delighted with the grey's first championship performance and began to look

MILTON'S FIRST GOTHENBURG WORLD CUP FINAL IN 1988. HE AND JOHN RECOVERED FROM A POOR SHOWING IN THE SPEED LEG TO FINISH EIGHTH OVERALL

AACHEN 1987: MILTON JUMPED A DOUBLE CLEAR ON HIS FIRST APPEARANCE IN THE NATIONS CUP AT THE RENOWNED GERMAN SHOW GROUND

forward to a tilt at the Europeans later in the season.

After a rest Milton was taken for a warm-up outing to the Oldcotes Charity show before heading, at the end of May, for Hickstead's Nations Cup meeting. There he won the Everest Double Glazing Stakes and was selected for the fourth team event of his career. Already he was becoming an indispensible member of the British squad and would make a total of eight appearances with official teams during the year.

Hickstead as it turned out was not a good show for the British. The strong American team of Anne Kursinski on Starman, Deborah Dolan on Albany, Joan Scharffenberger on Victor and Katie Monahan Prudent on Special Envoy swept to a devastating victory, only the second time in show jumping history that an all-female team had won a Nations Cup. So superior were they to the rest of what was widely regarded as one of the strongest fields ever seen at the Sussex showground that Katie, starting at number four for the first time in her life, was not required to jump at all. Their success cheered up their team leader George Morris no end. The 49-year-old Olympic and Pan American Games veteran was watching on television in nearby

Cuckfield Hospital, where he had been taken on the second day of the show after breaking two vertebrae in his neck in a horrifying fall over one of Hickstead's permanent obstacles, an oxer incorporating a privet hedge.

Britain's quartet of Harvey Smith, Janet Hunter, Michael Whitaker and John could manage only a distant fifth place though Milton again acquitted himself well and was the only horse in the team to produce a clear round. He had four faults in the first round at the vertical going out of the treble but was clear, only just outside the time, on his second appearance. His efforts, however, were to no avail and Germany, France and Holland all finished on better scores than the host nation.

Milton's next port of call was the Royal International in mid-June where John hoped to retain the King George V Gold Cup. His 1986 winner, Ryan's Son, was now 19 and in deference to his years was being given only the occasional, carefully selected outing to supply him with a bit of interest in his old age. Milton jumped in the *Daily Mail* Cup on the opening day at Birmingham, making just one mistake at the last fence, before tackling his first King George the following day. And how well he went. He was one of five horses to record double clears which took him through to the timed jump-off. Had he not been handicapped by an early draw, he might well have won it.

Starting in second place John had no option but to push on in order to set those who followed a tough time to beat. Unfortunately he pushed on perhaps just a fraction too much and Milton hit the final fence. Second last to go, Frenchman Hubert Bourdy, who three years later would be riding Milton as a finalist in the World Equestrian Games, went deliberately slowly and was rewarded with the first clear round. But he had taken nearly ten seconds longer than Milton, and Malcolm Pyrah, with the benefit of the final position in the draw, knew that he could go just as carefully with the reliable Towerlands Anglezarke and still win. He did so with more than five seconds to spare – his second King George in three years. Milton, easily the fastest horse in the jump-off, took third place. Malcolm and Anglezarke, once more with the benefit of a late draw, were again in unbeatable form in the Grand Prix. Milton, who finished fifth, was most unlucky to miss the jump-off: John had taken things too leisurely in the first round and incurred an expensive quarter of a time fault.

The following week Milton made his Aachen Nations Cup debut. The heavy rain, which had been playing havoc with European equestrian events all season, followed the show jumpers to Germany and threatened to wreck the 50th official international show to be held in this world-famous arena. Some of the early competitions were transferred to the nearby indoor riding hall. But this renowned event attracts such huge daily crowds – in excess of 40,000 whatever the weather – that it would have been unthinkable to hold the big contests, such as the Nations Cup and the Grand Prix, in a small arena with so little seating for the public. Consequently they went ahead on the rain-sodden turf.

Despite the difficult conditions underfoot the horses coped pretty well. Milton jumped an immaculate double clear in the team event to help lead Britain to a jump-off against the all-powerful Americans. A third clear round would have given victory to the British but Milton made one error and the two teams, finishing on equal scores, had to be divided by time. The United States won by a margin of over nine seconds.

Good placings at the Hickstead Dubai meeting were followed by another Nations Cup show, at Falsterbo in Sweden. Milton had a fence down and a quarter of a time

THE VICTORIOUS BRITISH TEAM IN ST. GALLEN 1987: MICHAEL WHITAKER, JOHN, MALCOLM PYRAH AND NICK SKELTON

fault in the first round and was left needing a clear in the second half if the British were to take the much improved Austrian team to a tie. John and the grey duly obliged. But for the second time in three weeks Britain was destined to lose a team event in a jump-off against the clock. The duos of John and Milton, and Michael Whitaker with Warren Point went clear, but the Austrians did even better, scoring three clear rounds from their four starters to give them a decisive victory. It was a historic occasion, too, since it was Austria's first team success since Nations Cups began back in 1909.

The show was also something of a historic occasion for Milton, for it was the second and last time that John ever competed with him in a Derby. He finished third behind Harvey Smith and Sanyo Shining Example, who were winning for the second successive year. Michael ensured that it was an all British affair by taking second place on Warren Point. Since then John has not risked Milton over a Derby course.

Dublin and Rotterdam came next on the agenda. At the former meeting Britain again finished frustrated runners-up in the Nations Cup, beaten by a comfortable margin by the home side. John and Milton were the only British pair to go clear in the first round and although Nick Skelton and his Dublin specialist Apollo and Michael with Warren Point both came back with clears after the break, by this time the Irish had gone into an unassailable lead and there was no point in starting Milton a second time, since his score could not affect the result.

At the Dutch show a few days afterwards Milton was one of only three horses to jump a double-clear round (Jappeloup and Winzer were the others) but again his efforts were to no avail. The Austrians, riding on the crest of a wave after their Falsterbo success, scored a decisive victory over the Germans and French, with the British quartet fourth. Milton's brilliance was, however, amply rewarded in the Grand Prix in which he produced three clear rounds and took the £6,000 first prize by a clear margin of two seconds. This time it was Jappeloup, back in fifth place, who was a shade unlucky not to feature in the shake-up, just as Milton had been in Birmingham. The French star had gone clear in the first two rounds, only to pick up a quarter of a time fault in each and so be deprived of a place in the jump-off. But the little horse was in just as good form as his bigger grey rival and the scene looked set for a truly vintage battle in the European Championships two weeks later.

St Gallen in Switzerland was the attractive venue for Milton's first attempt at a European title. Again inclement weather did its best to ruin things. It rained heavily for half of the opening championship class and throughout the morning of Nations Cup day but the organisers and course builder, former Swiss international rider Paul Weier, coped admirably. Most people felt that the show executive did not deserve the criticsm levelled at them by the defending champion Paul Schockemöhle, who was said to have given an interview condemning both the show and the ground conditions and who subsequently pressed for a 24-hour postponement of the team final to allow the ground to dry out.

Britain's mild-mannered team manager Ronnie Massarella spoke for virtually everyone else when he said, after the Nations Cup, that he believed the organisers had done a tremendous job: 'Obviously when you get weather conditions like this morning's it's difficult. But if the German team had got a postponement, it would only have delayed the inevitable – they were never good enough to win it.'

Ronnie had always maintained that his 'boys', Nick Skelton, Michael Whitaker, Malcolm Pyrah and John Whitaker, would retain the title which they had won two years previously at Dinard and how right he was. Jumping in that order, all four went clear in the opening speed class to finish in the top twelve and put Britain ahead of the French in the team standings. Nick and Apollo, who finished runners-up in the first crucial leg, were marginally faster than Milton. Malcolm and Anglezarke were ninth and Michael with his brilliant but somewhat enigmatic mare, Amanda, were in 12th position.

The class was won by Pierre Durand and Jappeloup and it was without doubt one particular manoeuvre which set them on the path to victory. Paul Weier's imaginative course provided a number of options, including an alternative fence at seven and the possibility – though it was only a possibility – of a time-saving turn from the double at eight to an upright at nine. It was a classic example of the need to know exactly your own particular horse's capabilities, to keep cool and to ride with absolute accuracy. Pierre, the man who once might have cracked under the pressure, measured the whole thing to perfection, turning his athletic little partner neatly inside the water jump, instead of going round it, and quickly setting up Jappeloup for fence nine.

Drawn 37th of the 43 starters, Pierre had time to assess the merits, or otherwise, of taking such a risk. Afterwards he said,

> Since most of the top riders, with the exception of John Whitaker, had already gone, and recorded good times, I had to do something, and since turns are not difficult for Jappeloup I decided to take the risk of turning in front of the water.

It paid off, and John, who jumped immediately after Pierre, considered that it won the French pair the class: 'I didn't think I could do that safely with Milton. I felt it was better to play safe and make sure I was in the first three or four. If I had to do it again, I would do the same.'

Pierre cited a fundamental difference between the two horses: 'In Rotterdam Milton won the Grand Prix because of his long strides. There was a two-stride combination which Milton was able to take in one stride. Jappeloup on the other hand is a shorter striding horse. If the course has many turns and short distances, it suits him, but when it comes to a course with long straight distances he is at a disadvantage.' John added that at the beginning of the competition he had thought the course would suit Milton quite well but by the time he actually came to jump it the mud had become deep, making it a much more difficult challenge than earlier.

Because of the rain that came down in torrents during the night and the following morning (the day of the Nations Cup, which together with the scores from day one would determine the team medals), the Ground Jury decided that, if necessary, at the end of the first round they would re-position any fences where the ground had been badly cut up. This was contrary to normal practice since a Nations Cup is designed to be run in two rounds over the same course, but it was a sensible decision and in the event three jumps were re-sited to make things safer for the horses. The time for the course was extended accordingly, though most riders found the allowances for both rounds rather too tight given the conditions, hence the prevalence of time faults.

The British squad, which had gone close but not actually won a team contest all year, chose St Gallen to get into top gear. So determined were they to defend their title successfully that the outcome became obvious from very early on. By the halfway stage of the Nations Cup they had extended their lead over France to three fences. By the end they were an almost embarrassing six fences ahead. In fact, once the third riders for each team had competed in the second round there was no way in which Britain could be beaten and in normal circumstances Milton would not have been required to start. However, in a championship it is the total scores from all three days which decide the individual placings so on this occasion John could not pull him out.

Apollo, who had been lame on arrival at St Gallen and was thought to have twisted his near-fore fetlock and bruised his sole, made a splendid recovery and apart from three-quarters of a time fault in the first round he jumped a fine double clear. Malcolm and Anglezarke had just one fence down in the second round, and Milton continued the tremendous form he had shown all season by putting in another double clear, though John slightly misjudged the second round – he admitted afterwards that he thought he was within the time but actually collected half a time fault.

Only the mare Amanda, clearly not enjoying herself at this show, caused the British supporters any anxiety, lowering as she did a total of five fences and also failing to complete either round inside the time. But the brilliance of the other three amply made up for her off day. Milton, in particular, had excelled himself. He had the lowest score of the entire competition and was poised to go into the final leg close up, in third place with a two-day score of 1.31 faults, 0.39 behind Apollo, who in turn was 0.17 behind Jappeloup. With the scores so close, none of the leading trio could afford a mistake.

After a rest day the third leg took place on a gloriously sunny afternoon over two different courses. John and Milton piled the pressure on the two leaders by jumping an impressive clear over the first big track. It moved them up into second place when Apollo made his first mistake of the show at fence two. Jappeloup responded with one of the best rounds of the championships, jumping from the sticky ground as if he had springs in his heels to retain his lead.

For the second round Paul Weier had posed one or two really difficult problems on his eight-fence course, among them number four, a pair of narrow white Helsinki gates. If Milton could be said to have a bogey fence it was this type of narrow, flimsy looking obstacle and sure enough it was his undoing – he gave the gate insufficient height, lowered it and collected four faults. As it turned out it was a mistake which cost him the championship.

John believes that because such obstacles are not very impressive looking Milton does not think about them enough: 'I wouldn't say that he's careless, more absent minded.' Like many top horses he probably finds it boring to tackle such unimposing looking fences and is busy looking for the next big oxer.

John also collected a time fault to end the three days on a grand total of 6.31, thus easing the pressure on Pierre, who started his last round in the knowledge that he had a fence in hand. However, the Frenchman immediately lost his advantage when Jappeloup rolled the front pole off the second fence. For a brief moment Milton was back in with a chance. But thereafter his little adversary was foot perfect, skipping round without further errors to give the French their first ever European title. Despite making two mistakes, Apollo managed to hang on to the bronze medal.

The closeness of the scores for the gold and silver underlined the comparable abilities of the two leading horses. They also emphasised the importance in these

St. Gallen 1987: John and Milton put up a spirited fight in the European Championships, but were defeated by their great rivals Pierre Durand and Jappeloup

championships, as in the World Cup, of that first speed class. On jumping performance alone there was nothing to separate the two horses. Time was the vital deciding factor. Although Milton's style of jumping has always made him rather slower through the air than Jappeloup, he readily makes up for that with his ability to lengthen his stride when required and to execute tight turns. So in the final analysis it all came back to Pierre's gamble on the first day. It was that in the end which swung the pendulum his way.

For John, it was particularly disappointing though he is too good a sportsman either to let it show or to let it get him down. But he must have begun to wonder if he was destined always to be the bridesmaid. Two years previously he had started the final day in the lead, only to slip to third. Two years before that at Hickstead he had won the silver. Balanced against his disappointment at not winning double gold was his immense satisfaction with Milton's performance over the three days. It had been a tough challenge and the bad ground had taken a lot out of the horses, but the grey had jumped really well throughout the show and that is what counted most.

Quickly putting his disappointment behind him, he headed for Calgary where the British team took up where it had left off in Rotterdam by finishing second in the Nations Cup, this time to the United States. Milton, now firmly established as the team's most reliable Cup horse, produced yet another faultless first round and did not start in the second because even a further clear could not retrieve the situation. He failed to get into the shake-up for the Grand Prix, finishing down in 21st place, though such is the incredible prize-money level at this show that even that earned him £450. Victory went to Ian Millar and Big Ben, who the following year would take Europe by storm in the World Cup.

Returning to Europe, Milton was consistently in the money in Stuttgart, where he has become the idol of the enthusiastic crowd, and at the Horse of the Year Show, where he narrowly missed out in the Leading Jumper of the Year to his old adversary Anglezarke. Again Anglezarke had the best of the draw in the jump-off and again Milton was beaten by a fraction of a second.

Re-crossing the Atlantic for the American fall circuit, John and Milton finished runners-up to Big Ben in the Toronto Grand Prix and produced yet another double clear in the Nations Cup in which, once more, Britain was beaten by the United States. It was Milton's eighth Nations Cup of the season. In two of them he not been required to start in the second round, so he had jumped a total of 14 rounds. With a fence down on only two occasions and three lots of time faults, he had jumped clear 10 times, double clear three times. It was a truly remarkable Nations Cup record. Little wonder that he was fast becoming known as one of the most consistent horses in the world.

After Olympia, where he won one class and was placed on every other occasion that he appeared, he went back to Yorkshire for his winter break. His winnings for the season totalled £91,742, almost £30,000 more than his nearest rival, Anglezarke.

CHAPTER 8

ONWARD AND UPWARD

For many people 1988 will live in the memory, as far as Milton is concerned, as the year in which Doreen and Tom Bradley stood firm by their decision not to permit him to go to the Olympic Games. Fortunately the storm of controversy which raged around him, and which is discussed in detail in Chapter 17, could not touch either his peace of mind or his jumping ability.

Horses are infinitely sensitive creatures and the reins of a bridle notoriously good transmitters of human fears and worries. How lucky, then, that Milton, the super champion, should have as his partner the peerless, professional John Whitaker. Not once during those long, difficult months did the horse pick up any tension from his rider, not even when the controversy reached its peak. The proof lies in his performance record for the year: on the Grand Prix circuit he reached even greater heights of brilliance and consistency than in the previous season. In France, Germany and Holland during the first two weeks in March he was unbeaten in six major classes. In the World Cup Qualifiers in Paris and s'Hertogenbosch he jumped six consecutive clear rounds to win the Volvo car at each show. For good measure he also won the Grand Prix in Dortmund. In the three weeks or so since his return to competition in Antwerp at the end of February he won in excess of £25,000. John finished runner-up to Pierre Durand in the European League of the World Cup, and headed for the final in Gothenburg at the beginning of April, with understandable hopes of improving on his performance of 12 months previously.

Britain's Alan Oliver, the former top international rider turned course designer, had provided the tracks this time and for the problematical first leg had given riders the option either of taking some risky short-cuts or of simply galloping round longer routes. Both options proved viable and the riders generally were full of praise for Alan Oliver's concept. Unfortunately, as John explained, the course did not suit Milton's style of jumping. Nor perhaps did he himself judge things all that well. In fact, it was very much a carbon copy of the first leg in Paris the year before.

Milton was drawn in the first half of the field of 45. Early on, three American riders had jumped clear rounds in under 60 seconds, including George Morris, now happily recovered from the serious neck injury he had sustained at Hickstead. Britain's Liz Edgar, winner of the Helsinki qualifier the previous October, had also got the measure of the course and had swept into the lead with Everest Rapier. Seeing how fast the course was riding, John understandably felt compelled to 'go for it'. But halfway round Milton hit the top of a set of vertical white rails coming off a bend. Desperate to claw back some time, John went for a really tight turn into the penultimate fence, an oxer – too tight as it turned out, because Milton had another

A PACKED HOUSE AT WEMBLEY WATCHES THE FAVOURITE CLAIM THE FIRST RUNNING OF THE WINNER-TAKES-ALL INTERNATIONAL MASTERS

rail down. Without those two mistakes his time would have placed him eighth. As it was he ended up down in 26th position and no one had ever pulled back from quite that far to trouble the leaders.

Afterwards John confirmed what he had thought when he walked the course: the fences were on the small side for Milton.

> He can jump a big Grand Prix course quite fast, but the speed I had to go in this class was faster than he's used to. Because he takes off slowly as well as being slow through the air, I have to try to make up time somewhere else. This time it didn't work.

Malcolm Pyrah, who was to figure in the shake-up the following day, agreed, saying that:

> In a Grand Prix jump-off you may think horses are going fast but compared to a speed class they're probably going about 5mph slower. It's difficult for a Grand Prix horse to go fast round a small course because he's not used to doing that. But you can't condemn a course just because it doesn't suit you.

Victory actually went to a horse who looks altogether too big to fly round a speed track in an indoor arena, Big Ben. One of the ante-post favourites, he had carried Ian Millar to individual and team gold medals in the 1987 Pan American Games. Despite the fact that Big Ben has such a naturally long, raking stride, Ian had opted to take some of the shortest routes on the course and in doing so it has to be said that he made the whole thing look ridiculously easy. Ben demonstrated his tremendous athleticism as he twisted and turned, kept his balance and gave each fence inches to spare. It was, undoubtedly his huge stride which finally won him the class.

Ian's compatriot, Laura Tidball-Balisky riding Quartz, Belgian-bred like Big Ben, demonstrated that a galloping-on approach to the course was also perfectly feasible on the right horse. She took the longer routes, kept up a relentless rhythm and finished runner-up in a time that was only 0.15 slower than Ian's, which proved just how cleverly the course had been devised.

The European Champion Pierre Durand, one of the other favourites, had decided to go for a steady clear with Jappeloup. His play-safe tactics looked likely to succeed until, that is, he reached fence eight, where he made an unlucky mistake. The obstacle was a straightforward enough wall but as Jappeloup jumped it Pierre knocked the upright with his boot, causing a brick to dislodge. His time would have been good enough to put him fifth but that unfortunate error cost him 12 places.

As usual, Milton was much more at home over the bigger fences in the second leg, in which he and his rival Anglezarke provided an all-British jump-off. Anglezarke, 17 years old and only lightly worked in the build-up to this show because Malcolm Pyrah's long-term aim was to go to the Olympics, was a bit 'ring rusty' on the first day. But he, too, evidently enjoyed getting his teeth into the challenge of a bigger track and according to his rider 'in the second round felt like he did ten years ago'. He was one of nine horses to go clear initially. Among the others were Big Ben, Jappeloup and Britain's Hungarian-born Joe Turi with his Olympia Qualifier winner Vital. However, all but Milton and Anglezarke faulted in the first jump-off by which time the fences were really testing.

The grey and the chestnut had battled out several exciting finishes over the previous 12 months and only a brave punter would have bet against Anglezarke in a jump-off against the clock, even if he did have to go first Malcolm reckoned that his horse's stride was a good 18in shorter than Big Ben's, but there was no horse better at maintaining his momentum over big fences at speed. True, he gave fence eight a bit of a rattle, but it stayed put and he was across the finish in the fast time of 36.27 seconds. Forced to put his foot down, John beat that by more than a second, though at the cost of hitting the second element of the double. But he had demonstrated that Milton can indeed jump quickly enough when the fences are big and this performance pulled him right up to equal tenth place. Malcolm, for his part, having finished day one in 18th, shot up into third.

Big Ben's equal fourth place with, among others, Jappeloup, was sufficient when added to his first-day win to ensure that he started day three with the coveted zero score. He had a clear fence in hand over the consistent Belgian pair, Philippe Le Jeune and Nistria, winners of the Antwerp qualifier at the beginning of the year. Nistria had finished fourth on the first day of the Final and tenth on the second.

Alan Oliver's big course for round one of the third leg again suited the true Grand Prix-type horse. It produced only five clear rounds. Big Ben could afford the one mistake which he made, but Nistria could not, and paid for his when a faultless performance by Jappeloup took the French challenger up from sixth to join him in equal second place. Milton, who also jumped a fine clear, edged up another three places.

The only mistake which the grey made in the second round came, significantly, at a narrow vertical, not unlike the Helsinki gate which had caught him out in the European Championships. But his total for the three days of 15.00 was good enough to place him eighth overall. Considering his hopeless situation on day one he had done very well indeed to figure among the top ten. When Jappeloup completed a magnificent double clear round it assured him of outright second place, as Nistria once more collected four faults. All that was left was for Big Ben to coast round to claim the Cup for Canada. He still had a fence in hand, but he made no mistake this time and wound up three days' tremendous jumping with a confident clear.

John gave Milton a break after the rigours of the World Cup, then came out and won an Area International Trial with him before going to the Hickstead Nations Cup meeting at the beginning of June. It was there that the wrangling over his non-

IN FULL FLIGHT AT
HICKSTEAD IN 1991,
WITH THE £21,000
GRAND PRIX PRIZE AT HIS
MERCY

availability for the Olympics reached its peak. Milton jumped a superb double-clear round in the team event, the only one of the entire competition. Ironically, at a time when he was, arguably, reaching his peak, it was to be his only official appearance for Britain that year. The selectors decided to bar him from the rest of the season's teams if they could not have him for the Games. This considerably restricted John's opportunities to jump him abroad. Riders are dependent on being officially nominated to an invited team or being given a personal invitation by the show itself, and such places are very limited at the big events. He did take him to two non-Nations Cup shows, Franconville and Zurich, and went extremely well in both, winning the Grand Prix at the latter.

Between Hickstead and Franconville Milton made an outstandingly successful visit to the Royal International. The lure of big prize-money overseas and, in normal seasons, the demands of the Nations Cup circuit, mean that top horses are rarely seen by their home fans. British audiences are lucky if Milton makes more than half a dozen appearances a year on home ground, so it is always gratifying to his connections if he goes well in his own country.

In Birmingham he kicked off in tremendous style by winning the *Daily Mail* Cup on the opening night, defeating John's brother, Michael, on Amanda, by nearly three seconds in the jump-off. Two nights later he had his second crack at the King George, in which he had been third the previous year. This time he had a more favourable draw in the jump-off, second last to go from the four finalists. John easily beat the time set by first man in David Broome on Countryman. But the last to go, Robert Smith with David Bowen's former mount Boysie, a pair who had tried in vain to catch Milton in the *Daily Mail* class, had their revenge. Robert, putting Boysie's considerable turn of foot to full use, cut more than two seconds off John's time to take the coveted trophy for a second time.

The following night though, it was Milton who stole the limelight as he finally turned the tables on his senior rival Anglezarke, the horse who had so often got his head in front when the two were matched against the clock. In the Everest Double Glazing Grand Prix, Anglezarke, going first of the four in the jump-off, went brilliantly clear to stop the clock in 33.70 seconds. Nick Skelton was also clear but well down on time with Grand Slam and it began to look as if the canny Malcolm Pyrah had provided too difficult a target. But John and Milton were having none of that. Turning and jumping with wonderful accuracy, Milton clipped half a second off Anglezarke's time, leaving John Brown and Sligo Supreme, the last to jump, a hopeless task. The crowd hailed the grey as the hero of the show, and no wonder: he had jumped seven rounds without touching a fence, ensuring that John won the leading rider award. Olympics or no Olympics, people just loved to watch him in action. Those who followed him to Wembley later in the year saw him perform in even more devastating style.

The near unbeatable form he showed at that year's Horse of the Year Show was probably due to an easy summer campaign. A trip to the Hickstead Dubai meeting in July and to Mondorf Les Bains in August were not exactly exhausting and he arrived at Wembley a fresh horse. By this time he was probably wondering why he had not seen his old friends and rivals for so long. Perhaps he was missing the adulation of the public. If he was, he lost no time in reminding everyone of his star status.

He easily beat a class field in the Rover Classic on his first appearance. He left them all trailing in his wake again in the feature event 24 hours later, the Norwich Union International. These successes qualified him, together with six other horses, for the Next International Masters. The brainchild of George Davis of Next (at that time John's sponsors) the Masters provided British show jumping with the biggest boost the sport had seen for many a year. It was a very long time since a major jumping event in this country had seen a capacity audience on the edge of its seats from the moment the first horse entered the ring. Devised as a winner-takes-all event for seven horses qualified by their performances in earlier competitions, it was run that first year over four rounds. The original idea had been that each rider, having drawn lots for the starting order, could choose to raise up to four fences on the course in each round and, provided they cleared that course, the prize-money kitty, starting at £8,000, would go up by £1,000 for each fence raised.

However, the more people thought about it the more it became clear that this might well lead to the competition finishing too soon – a real anticlimax if too many horses were knocked out in the early rounds, because the course becomes too big too soon. Therefore, it was decided instead that each rider should be allowed to raise only one fence of his or her choice in each round. This provided a contest that was easy to understand and exciting – both vital considerations when it came to spectator-appeal. It also meant that tactics played a big part. For example, Milton's great forte is his ability to clear huge spread fences, so obviously John opted to make one of the oxers higher and wider each time, safe in the knowledge that this would not trouble his horse. His rivals, on the other hand, undoubtedly felt that the best way of finding a chink in his armour was to keep raising one of the verticals, provided of course that they themselves had a horse with the necessary talent to clear them.

The wily David Broome chose each time to raise the last fence, an upright of planks. In the third round this ploy successfully dismissed two Olympic gold medallists from Germany, Ludger Beerbaum on Amigo and Franke Sloothaak on Sandro, as well as Austria's Thomas Frühmann on the powerful stallion Grandeur. David, riding Countryman, cleared the planks each time, and was one of only three to go through to the fourth and final round. Countryman just managed to clear the planks at six-feet high and then David had a nail-biting wait as Nick Skelton with Serenade came in for his final attempt. Serenade's chance went at the second element of the double, an oxer which John had raised in each of the preceding rounds. This left the prize waiting for John. Leaving the double alone this time, he increased the size of another oxer, fence four. Despite twice losing his stirrups and actually stopping before approaching fence four to get them sorted out again, he steered the incomparable

Milton safely round. As the pair landed clear over the planks the whole of London must have heard the cheers. Since the pool now stood at £25,000, it made it the joint-biggest prize in the country, equalled only by the Hickstead Derby.

The one slightly sour note at the end of a brilliantly entertaining competition was that Countryman, who had like Milton been faultless throughout, should be pipped at the post virtually as a result of John having the better draw. If it had been the other way about, and Countryman had been last to go, there was no reason to suppose that he would not have jumped another clear round. But David was philosophical in defeat, likening the class to a game of poker. And, of course, it had to be remembered that all the riders had agreed to compete under the rules as they stood.

John sportingly came up with the idea of donating £3,000 of the kitty towards consolation prizes for the other contestants. Next decided to match this, and so each of the six losers went home with £1,000. For Dutchman Albert Voorn on the aptly named Wembley it was a most profitable exercise: he had won £1,000 by jumping only one clear round over a five-fence course. Not a bad few minutes' work!

Milton came out again on the final evening to a tumultuous reception and only narrowly missed winning the Grand Prix, in which victory went, by less than three-quarters of a second, to Franke Sloothaak riding Aramis. But second place was sufficient to ensure that John and Milton earned the title of Leading Show Jumper of the Year. Traditionally decided by a single competition on the Wednesday evening of the show, the title this time was awarded, by way of a change, to the highest points winner in the international classes throughout the week. Milton not only headed the points table, he amassed by far and away the biggest prize purse ever gleaned from the Horse of the Year Show: a staggering £36,100.

His triumphant progress continued a couple of weeks later in Stuttgart, a show where the enthusiastic and knowledgeable crowd has taken him to their hearts as if he were their local hero. From four starts he notched up one third place, one second and two wins, the latter in the two plum classes of the week. The first was the German Masters, for which the top prize was a Mercedes. The second was the Grand Prix.

Ever onward and upward, he went to three of the early World Cup competitions of the 1988-89 winter season, Amsterdam, Bordeaux and Brussels, where he finished the qualifiers in, respectively, fourth, seventh and first places. On the last occasion he won another Volvo to add to the two he had collected in Paris and s'Hertogenbosch earlier in the year. He was beginning to run out of garage space. Despite the interruptions to his overseas campaign caused by the rumpus over the Olympics, Milton would finish the season with an unprecedented £147,820 to his credit, nearly three times as much as runner-up Apollo. All in all, it had been by any standards a dramatic year. Before it was over, there would be one more dramatic event in Milton's life, one which came close to bringing about a totally unplanned change of ownership.

CHAPTER 9

A BRUSH WITH DEATH

It was December 19, 1988: Doreen and Tom Bradley's 48th wedding anniversary. They had spent the day, like the four previous ones, enjoying the unique atmosphere of the Olympia Show Jumping Championships, London, where Milton was naturally one of the chief attractions. This traditional end-of-year event, part serious horse show, part pantomime, always boasts an outstanding field of international riders, the biggest carrot being the World Cup qualifying round, which carries lucrative prizes, headed by the usual Volvo and valuable European League points for all the placed riders. 1988 was no exception. John and Milton were leading the British contingent, which included John's brother Michael, Nick Skelton, David Broome and Joe Turi. Spearheading the overseas attack were three Seoul Olympic team gold medallists, Germany's Ludger Beerbaum, Franke Sloothaak and Dirk Hafemeister; there was the young Belgian star Ludo Philippaerts as well as top riders from eight other countries.

The imperturbable John had set himself a punishing schedule. He planned to partner Milton in the World Cup class on the Saturday afternoon. Immediately afterwards he was to fly to Grenoble where he had another horse, Gammon, waiting to take part in the £10,000 Renault Grand Prix (he duly won it and only narrowly missed heading the overall points table in the Renault Jump Series for which the top prize was a £20,000 car, the *Cherokee Chief*.) Then he would fly back on the Monday morning in order to prepare Milton for the Crosse and Blackwell Grand Prix at Olympia that evening.

Milton thrilled his fans by jumping two faultless rounds in the World Cup on the Saturday but, largely because of the disadvantage of his number-one draw in the jump-off, he was edged out on time faults. He finished less than half a second behind Ludo Philippaerts on Darco, and 700ths of a second behind runner-up Thomas Frühmann of Austria on Grandeur. So it was Ludo who drove off with this particular car while John prepared to make his dash for the plane to Grenoble in pursuit of another.

The Bradleys had decided not to go in for any celebrations on their anniversary. It had been a hard week, Doreen recalls. They had been to Brussels to see Milton jump, lost their luggage on the way back, had a couple of days at home, then driven down to Olympia. Doreen Bradley had risen early on the Monday morning to meet John off the plane from Grenoble to take him back to Olympia, and both she and her husband were conscious of the fact that it would be midnight before they set off on the long drive home. Little did they imagine it was to be a journey they would not complete.

After watching Milton in the Grand Prix, he qualified for the jump-off but hit

two fences to finish sixth behind Walzerkönig, the Bradleys climbed into their car – a Volvo estate. It was a 'Milton car', won at an earlier World Cup show. It had done only 700 miles and Doreen, driving the first stint, planned to take things steadily.

They had agreed that they would change over at Toddington services on the M1, she remembers. 'We did change at Toddington – but not in quite the way I meant. I know that I was driving at about 63mph because I had told Tom that I was going to have to put the speed up. I was on the inside lane and was being roughed up by a big lorry with a trailer on the back. To this day I don't know whether perhaps the lorry took a side sweep at me – but the next thing I knew I was on the embankment.'

Tom had nodded off at the time and he thinks the most likely explanation is that his wife did, too. 'If I did, it could only have been a momentary thing. I remember the car going up and then realised that it was going to tip over, so I started to turn to try to straighten it out.' It was only then that she saw it: right in front of her the concrete arch of a bridge. If the retaining wall of the bridge had been a yard further away, Tom reflected, she'd have got away with it. It wasn't and she didn't.

Doreen remembers nothing about the impact. The next thing she knew, there were arc lights overhead and she was wondering where the fresh air was coming from. It was coming through the top of the car which by this time had been cut away by rescue workers. They managed to extricate Tom, shaken though miraculously undamaged, without too much difficulty. His glasses were scratched but still on his nose, and his spare pair were still in his cardigan pocket, unbroken. His wife was another matter and it took much longer to free her.

> I remember a policeman getting so cross because the seat belt wouldn't come undone and then when they tried to move my seat back to lift me out they couldn't. I sit fairly far forward anyway when I'm driving and to make matters worse we'd folded down the back seat – it was Christmas and we had all sorts of goodies to take home with us and thought it would be easier to pack that way.

The impact had caused the folded-down back seat to become jammed into the rear of the front seats. When eventually they did prise her out, they 'shifted the body' as Doreen wryly puts it, to hospital in Luton where the catalogue of injuries made gruesome reading. Putting her feet out at the moment of impact had caused compaction of both heels and given her two broken ankles. When the front of the car jammed down on her legs, one snapped, the other 'needed returfing'. One knee was badly smashed and had to be pinned together, her plastic replacement hip had come adrift from its moorings, she had a punctured lung, which collapsed, a cracked sternum and two broken arms. Plus sundry cuts and bruises. She was not expected to live through Christmas.

The surgeon, Mr Dyson, who painstakingly put the body back together again told Tom that it was only her temper which pulled her through: if she hadn't been so angry, she wouldn't have lived.

Doreen wished that she could be moved nearer home, to Northampton, but it was out of the question. Later she learned that if she **had** to smash herself up it was not a bad move to do it near Luton, since the hospital there has one of the best accident units in the country. It certainly lived up to its reputation. That she pulled through at all was a tribute to the skill of her surgeon and all the nursing staff who cared for her. Mr Dyson gave her no false hopes, warning her that she might never walk again. It was three months before she went home.

Undoubtedly the thought of travelling again to see Milton jump did much to strengthen her resolve to become mobile and not end up confined to a wheelchair. But it was certainly far from easy and the odds were stacked against her. Polio had left her with one leg an inch shorter and several inches smaller round the thigh than the other – 'I never did look much good in a bikini.' It was largely because of this original unevenness that her hip had become worn and had to be replaced. Now, not only was the affected leg less muscular and therefore slow to mend, she also had virtually no heel at all on her right foot. Only through an enormous amount of dogged determination, backed up by specially designed shoes and a pair of crutches, did she slowly, and painfully, begin to regain her balance and learn to walk again.

Now, remarkably, she can and does walk unaided, though she always takes a crutch with her when she travels. Nick Skelton whimsically dubbed it 'Mrs Bradley's rapping pole'★ because one day some of the riders borrowed it to help construct a practice fence. Doreen finds her 'rapping pole' essential for safety in public places such as airports because it makes other people more careful and less likely to bump into her. Otherwise she makes no concession to her brush with death and speaks lightly of her fight back to fitness. 'Well, you've got to live, haven't you, when the surgeons spend that length of time on you?'

Milton has won several more Volvos since the accident, but the Bradleys do not drive them. They prefer a Mercedes. Milton has obligingly been known to win the odd one of those, too.

It was July before Doreen and Tom Bradley saw their horse jump again and by that time a good deal had happened.

★Used in training to rap a horse's legs in order to encourage him to lift them higher on future occasions. An illegal practice at shows under BSJA and FEI rules.

CHAPTER 10

MILTON VERSUS BIG BEN

While Doreen Bradley was still languishing in hospital, Milton began his usual tour of the early World Cup events. After finishing fifth in the qualifier at s'Hertogenbosch and a very close runner-up to Thomas Frühmann and Grandeur in Paris, he went to Dortmund where he won the Grand Prix and thence to Geneva. There he defeated virtually all the best horses in Europe to take home yet another Volvo. It was one of the hottest qualifiers of the season and Milton won by a clear three seconds. In Antwerp the following week he again jumped by far the fastest round in the jump-off though on this occasion he lowered a rail and had to be content with fifth place. However, he had earned so many points during his winter campaign, that John emerged the winner of the European League, his first points victory since 1982-83.

The final was scheduled to take place in Tampa, Florida, in early April. It was only the second time that it had been awarded to the United States and there was a certain amount of apprehension about it on the Europeans' part because the 1980 event in Baltimore had not exactly been a resounding success from an organisational point of view. Sadly, the 1989 show did not get off to a good start, either.

The lead-up to the first leg was marred by controversy over the quarantine restrictions imposed on incoming horses from Europe, which could have been construed as giving the North Americans an unfair advantage. Normally any horses going into Florida are required to be routinely tested for piroplasmosis, a blood disease mainly transmitted by ticks. Those found positive are refused entry. As some horses from France and Holland carry the disease there are one or two riders who would have been automatically banned from competing in the final. Rather than have that happen the World Cup organisers asked the United States Department of Agriculture if they would be prepared to waive the piroplasmosis tests. The request was granted but only on condition that all the European horses, who would be travelling out together on the same plane, went into quarantine upon arrival in Tampa, whether or not they were carriers of the disease. A special quarantine facility would be provided on the showground.

It seemed a fair compromise and was accepted; the World Cup Director, Max Ammann, believed that the horses would be released from quarantine before they started competing. It was not until nearly the end of March that he was notified that this was not, in fact, the case and that the horses would have to be kept in quarantine conditions for the duration of the show. This meant their living in stuffy, enclosed barn-type stabling and being exercised only in the indoor arenas.

It was hardly surprising that many of the European riders became somewhat disgruntled. It was not so much that they objected to the stabling and exercising areas per se. These were not much different from those experienced by horses like Milton at any European indoor show, though in view of the very warm weather in Florida – it was in the 80's daily – it would have been refreshing for them to have been allowed out in the fresh air. But the sense of prevailing injustice went deeper than that. The other finalists, from the Americas and Australasia, were enjoying cooler, open stabling and, more importantly, unrestricted outdoor exercise facilities.

Some of the European visitors stated quite openly their objection to a system which forced one lot of riders to school their horses under the constant supervision of the arena stewards, while those whose horses were not quarantined could wander over the showground wherever and whenever they chose. This, they hinted darkly, was an open invitation to the unscrupulous to indulge in malpractices such as rapping (see previous chapter), or 'poling' as it is known in the United States. 'Poling' is an accepted and perfectly legal training aid in the States, though within the confines of this show, run under the rules of the International Equestrian Federation, it was banned. However, the area available to riders on the Florida State Fairgrounds was too extensive for the stewards to be able to see what was going on behind every tree.

The organisers listened courteously to the grievances of the European riders and wisely decided thereafter to restrict everyone to the same exercising regime – ie indoors. The quarantined horses' stabling was also improved by the installation of fans and the provision of net screens which made it possible for the big doors at the end of the barn to be kept open. Things were looking up.

All that remained was for the ground in the arena to be improved, and technical delegate Arno Gego, Aachen's vastly experienced course designer, quickly had that attended to. During the warm-up classes riders had complained that the surface was too loose and was shifting under the horses' feet. Horses jumping late, particularly in a speed class, would be at a distinct disadvantage. It turned out that the surface, shavings on top of limestone screenings, needed watering and rolling. These problems were finally sorted out more or less satisfactorily and on the Wednesday evening the 11th running of the Volvo World Cup got underway with most of the ruffled feathers smoothed down.

Milton had stood up well to the long journey. After the warm-up class John reported that his partner was fit and fresh. The stabling and exercise arrangements would not, he felt, adversely affect his jumping performance though it would, he admitted, have been nice if the horse could have had gone out into the open air 'to see the flowers and the trees'. But John, never one to complain, was intent on getting on with trying to win the World Cup. He had gone to Tampa determined not to make the same mistakes in the speed leg three years running. And after walking the course, designed by the renowned former United States Equestrian Team trainer, Bertalan de Nemethy, he set himself a target of a clear round in 61 seconds. Milton, starting in 26th position in a field of 47 was clear in 61.75 and went into the lead. John was satisfied. The handful of British supporters were jubilant. However, their joy was rather short-lived for the very next horse in was the Cup holder Big Ben and he cleared the 12-fence track in an incredible 58.39 seconds. Nevertheless, it was John's best start ever. He finished the day in a very gratifying third place, the US rider Rodney Jenkins on Playback having recorded a clear in 60.98 to divide the two favourites. (Jenkins, whose consistent performance throughout the final would give him overall fourth place behind his compatriot George Lindemann on Jupiter, was later removed from the prize list after Playback failed a dope test.)

After the speed class John thought he could have gone faster but he had not wished to take any chances. The ground, he reported, was still moving slightly under the horses' feet and would have favoured the earlier horses. The highly partisan crowd were clearly impressed by their first view of Europe's wonder horse. His jumping style drew gasps of admiration. One new fan said he reminded her of a carousel horse. It helped make up for the disappointing performance of the host nation's own favourite, Gem Twist. On this occasion the American horse, ridden as usual by Greg Best, did not look like an Olympic medallist, refusing a fence early in the course and hitting two others to finish way down in 28th place.

In the absence of Jappeloup, whom Pierre Durand had not qualified for this final, the scene looked set for a battle between Canada and Britain, and so it turned out – though not before John had given his supporters a horrible fright during the first round of the second leg when it seemed he had thrown his first-day advantage straight out of the window. Bert de Nemethy's courses are always technically demanding, and it was in changing his mind about his approach that John incurred an expensive four faults and half a time fault early in the competition.

Fence two, a narrow black gate (which might have caught out Milton in the past but caused him no problem now) was followed by a 180° turn to a line of fences down the long side of the arena which required very accurate riding. Fence three, an oxer with a water ditch in front, came soon after the corner. De Nemethy had placed a one-stride double of verticals beyond it at a tricky distance. When walking it John had decided to ask Milton to take three long strides; for once, watching other riders tackle the problem first proved to be a mistake.

After seeing several go for three strides and get their horses into trouble, John at the last moment decided to ask Milton to fit in four very short ones. It proved impossible for the big grey to compress himself so much and he caught the first set of planks with his front legs. This stopped him in his tracks so effectively that it looked for a breathless moment as if he might be forced to jam on his breaks. But he succeeded in cat-jumping over the second element with commendable agility and John was quick to acknowledge afterwards how well his partner had done to get them both out of trouble. The rest of the round was a model of accurate riding but the incident cost John 4.50 faults and with five riders jumping clear and another 12 finishing equal sixth on four faults, he ended the class in 18th place. It was fortunate for him that many of the four-faulters had finished down the field on day one and so Milton was still well up in fifth place overall after the first two days.

Continuing his relentless progress, Big Ben emerged the winner of this competition, run as usual over one round followed by two jump-offs. Of the five initial clears only he and the French horse Oscar Minotière, the mount of Philippe Rozier, were clear again to go through to the jump-off against the clock. Big Ben, first to go, was very fast but collected four faults at a big brown oxer coming out of a corner, which proved to be his only mistake of the entire show. Philippe Rozier decided to try for a slow clear, but Oscar hit the same oxer and was more than four seconds down on the clock to finish runner-up.

WORLD CUP FINAL 1989: MILTON FINISHED RUNNER-UP TO THE CANADIAN STAR BIG BEN

With a half-decent placing in the first leg, the Frenchman would have been up among the leaders at this stage. As he approached the first fence, an arena official walked across his path. Swerving to miss the official, he had no chance of jumping the fence and had to circle and come in again. It cost him many seconds and caused him to incur time faults. An objection looked in order, but the French *chef d'équipe* Patrick Caron advised against it, believing that it would not be successful. So despite jumping a terrific clear round poor Philippe found himself in 26th place.

The courses throughout the show really made the riders think. Ian Millar, who has always admired de Nemethy's work, even when he has been defeated by it, considered the first round of the second leg a fabulous track:

> Bert uses water hazards and verticals better than any course designer I've ever seen . . . there was lots of size, for sure, but the course had tremendous subtleties. You had to have a plan and a horse that was trained well enough to allow you to execute your plan – a brave, super-careful horse.

John echoed these sentiments after the third and final leg in which, he said, the course again called for a careful horse with abundant scope. Milton, like Big Ben, proved once more that he has both qualities and this time there were no last minute changes of plan by his rider to unsettle him.

The two rivals were the only horses, from the 34 coming forward to contest the last day, who mastered the fences twice without error. By the halfway stage, Milton had pulled up into third place overall, behind Big Ben and Playback. If John had not slightly misjudged the time in the second round, in his determination to leave the fences standing, Milton would have been joint-winner of the class with Big Ben. As it was he finished with a quarter of a fault and in second place. But his total for the three days of 10.75 faults (compared with Ian Millar's zero score) ensured him second place overall. It was the best British performance in a world cup final for five years.

For their part Ian and Big Ben wrote themselves into the record books by winning the Cup for a second time and in the most invincible style. It was fitting that they should receive their trophy from FEI President HRH Princess Anne ('Her Royalness' as the *Tampa Tribune* put it), whose first-ever visit to Florida had caused quite a stir.

If John was disappointed at finishing second, he gave no indication of it. At the post-prize-giving press conference he described Ian's performance as 'immaculate'. But when asked which horse he thought was the greater, Milton or Big Ben, he said, 'I wouldn't like to say – but I wouldn't swap Milton for Big Ben.'

CHAPTER 11

CHAMPION OF EUROPE

Milton went back to Yorkshire for a well-earned rest before the build-up to his next objective: the European Championships. For his return to the international circuit John took him to Cannes towards the end of May where he defeated a strong line-up of Continental starters to win the valuable Grand Prix with the only triple-clear round. A week later he was back on home soil for the Hickstead Nations Cup meeting. He jumped a double-clear round for the second successive year but the British team's performance was still not good enough to prevent the Edward, Prince of Wales Cup, from going abroad again. This time the French took the honours, ahead of the United States, with the host nation only third. Team manager Ronnie Massarella attributed the blame to three rider errors in the first round. The American former Olympic champion Joe Fargis won a fiercely contested Grand Prix on Mill Pearl, with Michael Whitaker on Mon Santa, and John on Milton, taking the minor placings.

A fortnight later, Milton arrived at Birmingham for the Royal International. John was performing one of his complicated 'how to be in two places at once' acts that week, commuting between England and Germany. The Aachen show, which had been brought forward to coincide with a local holiday, clashed with the Royal International. Since John was an indispensable part of the British team – even without Milton – he planned to come home to jump the grey on the opening night at Birmingham and then to dash over to Aachen for Friday's Nations Cup. To complicate matters further, it was his intention to return to Birmingham for the Saturday performance; then on the Sunday to compete in the Grand Prix at both shows, the German one in the afternoon and the British in the evening.

It was a pretty successful exercise, too, at least at the beginning. Milton won the Midland Bank Trophy at the Royal International on the Thursday and the next day the British team were victorious in the Aachen Nations Cup for the first time since 1981. Both John on Gammon, who had won the tough Hamburg Derby a few days previously, and Joe Turi on Kruger, jumped double clears.

Back in Birmingham on the Saturday John won the knock-out competition with San Salvador before taking Milton into the King George V Gold Cup. The field that year was small and, it has to be said, rather sub-standard and Milton not surprisingly was made the even-money favourite by the bookmakers. He looked the winner, too, after completing two clear rounds and then a third in a fast time in the jump-off against the clock. But, unfortunately for John, his brother Michael chose this moment to hit form with a horse normally associated with the puissance: Didi.

With only the Belgian-owned stallion to follow him in the jump-off, Milton, it seemed, had all but inscribed his name on the trophy. Even Michael did not give himself much chance, saying that he had only entered the stallion because his new mount Mon Santa was suffering from pulled muscles in his back. However, no one told Didi that puissance winners are not supposed to be able to jump Grand Prix competitions against the clock. He twisted his way round the course in the most breathtaking style, giving little hint of his reputedly suspect steering, and snatched victory from under the nose of his more famous rival by nearly two and a half seconds.

After that salutory experience John flew back to Germany but was out of luck in the Aachen Grand Prix, won by Franke Sloothaak and Walzerkönig. The Yorkshireman's subsequent return to the Royal International was fraught with problems. The flight he had intended to take from Brussels to Birmingham was delayed by nearly two hours so he had to fly to Manchester instead and do the last lap of the journey by road. Milton was drawn number two in the Grand Prix but the Ground Jury gave John dispensation to start last if, indeed, he arrived at all.

Against all the odds he did turn up, with about ten minutes to spare, though all was in vain as it turned out. Perhaps, at last, the travelling and tiredness were beginning to catch up with him. John is well known for being the most laid-back character, snatching an hour's sleep wherever he can, in airport lounges, in taxis, in the horsebox. But even he must have been beginning to feel the strain. Whatever the reason, Milton made an uncharacteristic mistake at the first element of the treble combination early on the course, which knocked him out of contention. Victory went, again, to Michael and Didi.

Jumping in the Zurich Grand Prix three weeks later, however, John and Milton demonstrated their true form by collecting the £27,000 first prize – an indication to the Continental riders that they were on song for the European Championships.

Rotterdam held a special attraction for Doreen and Tom Bradley for it was from there, exactly a decade earlier, that Caroline and Tigre brought home a team gold medal. Although Doreen was barely mobile at this stage following her car smash she was determined not to miss the 1989 Championships. This, the show jumping world agreed, would probably be Milton's best chance of winning the gold medal that John Whitaker had found so elusive. Jappeloup, Milton's conqueror in St Gallen, was now 15 and no longer improving, whereas Milton, two years his junior, was at his peak.

Doreen Bradley confesses to disliking the three-stage championships because they take so much out of a horse: 'Every time Milton's been asked to do one he's done it, but you cannot go on asking.' Nevertheless, there was no way she would be absent from the ringside on Thursday, August 17, when the curtain went up on what would be the finest achievement of Milton's career so far. He had looked in great heart on entering the arena for the warm-up class the previous day. John had popped him over the first seven fences and then retired so as to conserve the horse's energies for the real thing.

The Bradleys had missed their horse's tremendous showing in Tampa – Doreen had only just been discharged from hospital – but of course they had been brought right up to date with the details. Both they and the entire British contingent were as confident as they could be, in the uncertain world of horses, that the speed class in Rotterdam would pose no problem for John and Milton. Gone were the days when a poor first-day placing would leave them with too much leeway to make up. John had a good draw, 29th of the 40 starters. Course designer Olaf Petersen did them no harm, either, by building a track that suited the true Grand Prix horses and was not just a scramble against the clock.

Faults were spread pretty evenly all around the course, though the penultimate double, a triple bar to an oxer, proved particularly influential. Michael and Mon Santa faulted here, at the triple bar going in, as did Joe Turi on Kruger. Nick Skelton and Apollo also had a fence down, an oxer at eight. In fact only eight horses were clear. Milton was one of them and, to the great satisfaction of his fans, he was the fastest. It was a good omen: Pierre Durand and Jappeloup had won the speed leg two years previously before going on to take the title. John was obviously both delighted and relieved. 'Probably the most difficult part is over,' he said: 'Whatever fences they build now, Milton is capable of jumping them.'

At the end of the first day the British team was well poised for a record hat-trick of victories. Before the speed competition Ronnie Massarella had said that his aim was to have all four riders in the top ten. Three of them managed it, John, of course, plus Nick (ninth) and Michael (tenth). Joe had unfortunately misjudged the time and with six seconds to add for that fence down was in 24th place. But with only the three best scores counting for the team running totals, Britain ended day one with a slight advantage over France, 8.35 faults to 9.41 (unlike in the World Cup the times for this speed leg are converted into faults immediately and subsequently added to those in the Nations Cup to give the team result). The Dutch were lying third with a score of 10.96.

Friday's Nations Cup course was not too demanding, but it did pose a number of rider problems. Gratifyingly for British supporters, in the first half, Apollo, Mon Santa and Kruger were all faultless. Both Joe Turi and Kruger's owner, Michael Bullman, had been confident after their first-day hiccup that their horse would go well in the Cup, and how right they were. He went to Rotterdam as the only British horse to have jumped two double clears in team events that season. His initial clear round on this occasion would play a vital role in the winning of the team gold medal.

John and Milton, as was customary, were the last to go for Britain. Since they could do nothing to improve the quartet's standing at the halfway stage (three clear rounds meant that the team already had a zero score) there was no pressure on John as far as the team standings were concerned. He could concentrate on maintaining his advantage in the individual ratings. But to everyone's astonishment, not least his own, something went wrong at the penultimate obstacle, a 1.60m upright coming out of a corner. Milton hit it in front and collected four faults. The grey superstar had achieved the unthinkable: the team's discard score.

By this time, Britain was poised to take that third gold medal, having gone into a two-fence lead over the French, who were now a couple of faults ahead of the Germans and Swiss. As the shrewd Ronnie Massarella had predicted, his 'boys' were not able to pull away from the improved Continentals as easily as they had done two years previously, but their performance was well up to expectations. Except, of course, in one quarter. John and Milton had slipped down to fifth individually. Michel Robert of France, runner-up to the British pair the previous day, had gone clear to take the

ROTTERDAM 1989: MILTON LOOKING TYPICALLY KEEN AND HAPPY AS HE MAKES LIGHT WORK OF A WINDMILL OXER

lead, ahead of the German Olympic bronze medallist Karsten Huck on Nepomuk, Switzerland's Thomas Fuchs on Dollar Girl (destined to be briefly a future inmate of John's stable) and Nick Skelton with Apollo.

Much now depended on the second round, and it soon became obvious that the horses were finding things more difficult. Only three clear rounds were jumped, compared with 12 in the first half. Liberal, ridden for Belgium by Evelyne Blaton, recorded the first, though this pair were over the time. The Swan, ridden for Switzerland by Walter Gabathuler, had the second and Mon Santa the third. By the time the third rider for each country had jumped, the British already had the team gold medal in the bag. They had maintained their lead over the French, who were unable this time to produce any clear rounds. Switzerland, Holland and Germany fought out a spirited contest for the bronze, the decision finally going to the Swiss.

In the battle for the individual championship, Mon Santa, with the only double clear, had pulled himself right up into the lead with a two-day total of 4.53, which meant that Milton had to go clear to stay ahead. But if his first round mistake had been surprising, what happened next had onlookers rubbing their eyes in disbelief: Milton put a foot on the tape at the water. Normally the safest of water jumpers, he had never been known to do it before. Asked afterwards to explain, John thought that over the years horses tend to get used to jumping water and realise that they can land

close to or actually on the tape without coming to any harm. John blamed himself for under-riding it. It was an expensive mistake for it had cost him his precious first-day advantage.

Something which took even longer to sink in was the fact that Britain could actually have won *without Milton*. However, his four-fault second round did count towards the final score, enabling the team to discard one of the eight faults to give them a three-fence winning margin over France. Anyway, as Ronnie Massarella was quick to point out, Milton's very presence in the team was in itself a great morale booster for the other riders.

So, Michael and Mon Santa were the new leaders, Milton was second on eight faults. Felix, ridden by Dutchman Jos Lansink, Lafayette and Nepomuk were all close behind. Walzerkönig, with a two-round total of four faults, was creeping closer, as was the defending champion Jappeloup. The French horse had virtually thrown away his chances in the speed leg when he appeared to be staring so hard at the odd-looking wings of what was an innocent enough vertical that he saw the actual fence only at the last moment. Unable to get airborne in time, he crashed through the top of it and ended the day in 19th place. The chances of his finishing among the medals looked very remote indeed. However, a clear first round in the Nations Cup, followed by two fences down in the second, was sufficient to bring him up to 12th and by the final day he was looking much more like the little hero from Seoul.

Saturday was a rest day for the Championship horses, which was just as well for the winning team. One or two of the riders, not to mention a number of team officials, looked distinctly delicate the following day, suggesting that they had celebrated their victory in some style the night before. By Sunday, however, they were fit and well and ready to go after more medals.

This was not the first time that the Whitaker brothers had vied for championship gold. They had been in a similar position in Dinard four years before, where John was leading and Michael second going into the last day. 'In the end I just managed to get a bronze and Michael got nothing,' John recalled. 'In Rotterdam I remember us talking about it and saying that as long as one of us won it would be all right.' The Whitaker boys have been genuinely friendly rivals since they were children. There never was any jealousy, something which they put down to the fact that there is a five-year age gap (and another brother) between them so there was never any fighting over the same pony. Now, though both obviously wanted to win, they were happy that there were two of them in with a chance.

Starting in reverse order of merit, the 20 finalists faced a bigger course than on the Friday and there were no clear rounds until Jappeloup came in. Just how good his performance was became evident when no one else went clear until Milton. The grey made no mistake this time at the 4.50m water. Indeed, he cleared the entire course like a true champion. This meant that Michael also had to go clear if he was to stay ahead of his brother. Mon Santa was faultless and only a fraction outside the time.

In the second and final round over a much shorter course, Walzerkönig, Nepomuk and Jappeloup jumped clear, though the latter was outside the time, to finish in fourth, fifth and sixth places, respectively. Felix could not afford a fence down if he was to give Holland her first individual medal since 1977. His rider Jos Lansink, like John a farmer's son who had grown up with ponies, was less experienced at international level than the Whitaker brothers. But he was more than ready for the challenge that day. Cool and stylish, he coped admirably with the pressure, coasting home with no jumping faults and only a fraction outside the time.

When the crowd had settled down after its excitement, it was John's turn in the

hot seat. Milton by now was really enjoying himself – perhaps he thought the ovation for Felix was a greeting for him. At any rate he certainly never looked like making a mistake and although he picked up half a time fault, it meant that he was assured of, at worst, the silver. John said afterwards how strange it felt standing at the ringside knowing that only his brother stood between him and his first championship title. He was torn between wanting to win himself and not wanting Michael to have a fence down. But it was not to be Michael's day. Having jumped safely through four rounds without a mistake, the strain finally began to tell on a horse who, when all is said and done, simply does not have Milton's near limitless scope. The distress signals went up at the fourth fence, which he rattled. At the fifth he took a pole off and it was all over. Milton was champion of Europe.

Jappeloup's half a time fault for the two rounds made him equal winner of the third leg with his old rival, and the outgoing champion and the new title holder made a fine sight as they took a final lap of honour side by side before the medal presentations.

It was a proud moment for Doreen and Tom Bradley as the British National Anthem rang out for the horse their daughter had produced and in whom she had had so much faith. For Mrs Bradley in particular, who had overcome considerable physical infirmities just to be there, it was a wonderful boost.

After his exertions in Rotterdam Milton had a short rest before making his annual trip to Calgary, where the European contingent routed the North Americans in the Nations Cup. Britain won, fielding the same four riders as in the European Championships, the Swiss were second and the Germans third. Milton polished up his Nations Cup reputation by jumping the only double clear.

He jumped another two clear rounds in the Grand Prix, too, but a quarter of a time fault denied him a place in the jump-off. On this occasion it was Michael's turn to have the last laugh. Mon Santa jumped the only triple clear to take the world's richest show jumping prize, worth a cool £87,000 to the winner that year.

It was during this show that the news came out about John and Michael losing their sponsorship with Next at the end of the year. They revealed that they had known about it shortly before the European Championships but in typical Whitaker fashion it had not been allowed to affect their performances. With gold and silver medals to their credit, not to mention the unique attraction which Milton represented, it seemed unthinkable that they would have long to wait for a new offer.

John and Michael were two of the select band of riders invited to compete in Bremen a couple of weeks later in the new German Classics, the brainchild of Paul Schockemöhle. Milton again jumped a double clear in the Grand Prix, only to be beaten on time by Greg Best and Gem Twist, who were gaining sweet revenge for their team having been unplaced in the Calgary Nations Cup. Confirming the Rotterdam form, Felix and Jos Lansink finished third. Second place carried a prize of more than £18,000 and Milton came away from the show with a win and three placings worth in excess of £20,000. He did even better a fortnight later at Wembley.

The Horse of the Year Show crowd had come to hail their conquering European hero and he did not let them down. He won the big class on the opening night, finished runner-up to Joe Turi on Vital on his next appearance on the Thursday, and led the field of seven qualified for the Next International Masters the following night. Before a capacity audience John and Milton outwitted and outjumped their rivals just as they had done the previous year. On that occasion they had the luck of the draw, but this time fate offered no such helping hand: they were drawn number two and going into the fifth and last round Milton still had a couple of very dangerous opponents to jump after him – Nick Skelton with Serenade and Franke Sloothaak with Walzerkönig.

John had seen the first of the four survivors, Jos Lansink and Libero, put the final planks up to a massive 6ft 1in and go clear to take the prize purse to £25,000. In the final round the rules permitted a rider to raise two fences if he wished, and John opted to increase the size of two oxers. With the course now valued at £27,000, Milton made it look ridiculously easy. He could afford to relax afterwards, but John then had to stand on the sidelines and wait to see whether he would have the prize purse snatched from him, just as David Broome had done 12 months before. He need not have worried. Nick Skelton raised the first fence and after rattling the second part of the double, a big oxer that John had increased in all five rounds, his partner, Serenade, finally came unstuck at the planks.

Franke, too, raised fence one, and Walzerkönig, jumping at his impressive best, looked as if he might just be in the mood to pick up the £28,000 on offer – only to take one of the front rails off the triple bar and with it £1,000 from the kitty. Ending as it did on a rather negative note, the competition still did not totally satisfy the purists, but a victorious Milton was just what the crowd had come to see and they cheered themselves hoarse as he came in to receive his cheque.

In the Grand Prix the next night, it was Franke's turn to gain revenge – his week had not been blessed with good fortune. Underlining just how vulnerable these valuable horses are even when they are not competing, Leonardo, the extraordinary jumper with whom Franke would set a world puissance record of 2.40m (7ft 10 1/2in) in 1991, had fallen while being exercised on the lunge and injured a foreleg. Then shortly before the start of the Grand Prix on the final night Franke was met by his groom with the news that Walzerkönig had injured himself in his stable and was lame – on the same leg as Leonardo.

With little hope of success, Franke switched to his third horse, Argonaut, and no one was more surprised than he to find himself carrying off the top prize in a high-class jump-off. Milton, with the last draw of the 12 horses involved, was in the best possible position to claim a great double. But he made his first mistake of the week at the penultimate fence. As it turned out, even if he had been clear, he would not have beaten the German horse's time; he finished fifth but still went home with £34,500 in his purse, only marginally less than in the previous year.

As usual, at the end of October John took Milton to Stuttgart, famous as a centre of the car manufacturing industry and for its attendant traffic jams. The colossal scale of the latter – the 'rush' hour seems to last all day and night – make the task of commuting from hotel to horse show something of an endurance test. Doreen and Tom Bradley once made the mistake of leaving the show to go into the town centre to shop. They very nearly failed to see Milton jump that evening, but they made no such mistake on the night of the German Masters that year. Milton was bidding for a

WHITAKERS DOMINATED THE 1989 EUROPEAN CHAMPIONSHIPS: JOHN FIRST, MICHAEL SECOND, THOUGH IT WAS A NEAR RUN THING

EDZARD REUTER, PRESIDENT OF DAIMLER-BENZ AG, FULFILLS HIS AMBIITON TO HAVE A RIDE ON MILTON

second consecutive victory, for which the prize was once again a Mercedes – their favourite car. To the delight of his many vociferous German fans, he collected his car, and looked more than usually pleased with himself during the presentation ceremony.

It was during this show that the President of the Board of Directors of Daimler-Benz AG, Edzard Reuter, confessed to a long-held ambition: to ride Milton. As he was an accomplished horseman John and the Bradleys decided that the risk to either party would not be too great and one day, before the crowds arrived, Herr Reuter enjoyed the thrill of a lifetime as he took the big grey for a spin round the empty arena. He now belongs to a select band of people who know how it feels to sit on the world's most famous show jumper.

Stuttgart was followed by Vienna, where he won a class and jumped three clear rounds in the Grand Prix to finish third on time behind Thomas Frühmann and Grandeur. Then at the beginning of December Milton headed for Bordeaux, there to meet up with the other members of the title-holding triumvirate, Olympic champion Jappeloup and World Cup winner Big Ben. Ian Millar was on a rare trip to Europe to receive the leading show jumper award presented to him by the publishers of *l'Année Hippique*. To make his trip worthwhile he had been invited to take in some of the indoor shows and had ridden Big Ben to victory in the Grand Prix in Stuttgart.

Pierre Durand did not start Jappeloup in the Bordeaux Grand Prix, saving him instead for the next day's World Cup Qualifier. So it was left to Milton and Big Ben to carve up the prize-money. In a thrilling ten-horse jump-off Milton, drawn seventh,

WINNING THE MIDLAND BANK TROPHY AT THE 1989 ROYAL INTERNATIONAL HORSE SHOW

completed a third clear round and easily bettered the target set by the French National Champion Hervé Godignon with Quidam. But Big Ben, who followed the British pair into the arena, was even faster, thanks to his ground-devouring stride. As in Tampa earlier in the year, it was Big Ben one, Milton two.

Ian predicted that the outcome would be different in the following day's World Cup class when John had the better draw. It certainly was. Jappeloup, looking very fresh after his day off, went out with a fence down in the first round, much to the

disappointment of his local crowd. Milton was clear first time but made an uncharacteristic mistake in the second round, when he jumped rather too far over the first part of the double and as a result hit the vertical on the way out. Big Ben went clear twice to go through to the jump-off but rolled a pole off the very last fence just when he looked assured of victory. His was the fastest round, but with four faults the way was now open for someone to win with a clear. That someone was Morgat's rider Hubert Bourdy, who put all his cards on a safe, slow round and was duly rewarded with first prize, the Volvo car.

Before returning home Milton took in the Frankfurt show where he avenged his Wembley defeat by beating Franke Sloothaak for the valuable Grand Prix, worth over £15,000 to the winner. Milton jumped a triple-clear round. Walzerkönig, now happily recovered from his leg injury, was the other contender in the jump-off in which he had a fence down.

The following week the Whitakers' expected new sponsorship deal was announced: Henderson Unit Trust Management were to back the brothers to the tune of just over one million pounds over a period of three years. It came as no surprise that their additional involvement in the sport, to include a number of national Grand Prix competitions and the annual National Championship, would also embrace the hugely popular International Masters at Wembley. Doreen and Tom Bradley were not best pleased at the prospect of their horse being called Henderson Milton. They feel, quite rightly in the opinion of most people, that the majority of sponsors' names do nothing to enhance a horse. 'We weren't consulted about it,' Doreen Bradley said, 'but we accepted it in the end.' They wanted Milton to stay with John and fortunately their horse, more than any other in the world, was at least instantly recognisable to his public whatever his commercial prefix.

His last appearance as Next Milton took place at Olympia. In the jump-off for the World Cup, a class he had still not managed to win on home territory, he jumped an impeccable clear round only to be beaten on time by the two horses drawn after him, first by Viewpoint (Philip Heffer) and then by Grandeur (Thomas Frühmann). For the second year running John set off immediately afterwards for Grenoble where he had Gammon waiting to take part in the Grand Prix. He failed to win it but by finishing runner-up in the Renault Jump Series points table, John came away with £15,000 to take his own total prize-money for the season to well over £300,000. Milton for his part finished runner-up to Walzerkönig in the Grand Prix at Olympia and wound up his year with yet another new British record: £216,029.

Undoubtedly, though, it was the European title which had given John, the Bradleys and the entire British show jumping fraternity the greatest satisfaction. Now Milton's name was inscribed in the record books not just as a phenomenally successful Grand Prix horse and winner of vast sums of money but as a double gold medallist at championship level.

JOHN LOOKING PENSIVE ON HICKSTEAD NATIONS CUP DAY IN 1989. HE AND MILTON JUMPED DOUBLE CLEAR ROUNDS ON THEIR HOME GROUND IN 1988, 1989, 1990 AND 1991

CHAPTER 12

BREAKING THE NORTH AMERICAN STRANGLEHOLD

Like all celebrities, Milton is in constant demand to make guest appearances. But like all athletes, his competition programme has to be mapped out with infinite care, week by week, month by month, and there is no way that John could take the horse to all the shows which would dearly love to have him. Nevertheless one such occasion did tie in conveniently with his seasonal warm-up outing: the opening of Arena UK, near Grantham in Lincolnshire, towards the end of February 1990.

This up-to-the-minute equestrian centre was created by Italian-born John Lanni, a relative of the Massarella family, who came to England as a boy and has enjoyed great success here as a show jumping rider, course builder and trainer. It was appropriate that Britain's most famous horse and rider should perform the official opening ceremony at this attractive new complex. The indoor shows regularly held at places such as Arena UK are where the foundations of many an international jumping career are laid.

With his customary spookiness Milton thought twice about allowing John Whitaker to get close enough to cut the ribbon at the opening ceremony, but all was well in the end and he was happy to do his bit by jumping the 'opening fence'. He went on to collect £100 for finishing fourth in the Grade A and B class. Thereafter he was quickly into his stride at his first international outing of the year, the World Cup show in Antwerp. He won one big competition and was runner-up in another, though he missed getting through to the jump-off for the World Cup Qualifer after faulting in the first round. But it was a different story in Paris a week later where he convincingly defeated Frank Sloothaak on Walzerkönig, Franke's compatriot Otto Becker on Lucky Luke, and Frenchman Eric Navet with Quito de Baussy, to take home his sixth Volvo. Within another week he had made it seven by winning in s'Hertogenbosch. In Gothenburg, where the European League came to a conclusion at the end of March, he finished equal fifth. He delighted his numerous Swedish fans by winning the Grand Prix for a second time. John again headed the League points table.

As the climax of the indoor season approached, all the predictions were that 1990 was to be Europe's year, that the stranglehold on the World Cup, established by the North Americans during the previous ten years, was at last about to be broken and that John Whitaker and Milton were to be the pair to break it.

It was certainly no impediment to Milton's cause that Big Ben, the outstanding winner of the 1988 and 1989 finals, was unable to try for a hat-trick of victories. Ben was recovering from an operation following an attack of colic. Although Ian

Millar had a second horse qualified, Czar, Dortmund was to be the Canadian's first indoor show with him – his chances of winning a third title looked slim.

As for the United States, their squad had begun to show signs that it was no longer the well-oiled machine we had come to expect during the past decade. One or two of the US League leaders had equine injury problems. Others had opted to stay away from the Dortmund final or to bring their second-string horses in order to save their top mounts for the forthcoming World Equestrian Games in Stockholm. The Europeans, justifiably as it turned out, favoured a bolder approach. Neither John Whitaker nor Olympic Champion Pierre Durand, to name but two, felt that aiming for both championships posed a problem, the time between them being quite sufficient for Milton and Jappeloup to have a breather.

It was on Milton that the mantle of favouritism inevitably fell. Everyone from the World Cup director to the humblest newspaper scribe was predicting victory for the grey. He had the advantage of being a couple of years younger than his arch-rival from France and had shown himself to be in sparkling form during his spring preparation. John, in retrospect, felt that the horse had probably peaked a little too soon the previous year, but he was sure he had him absolutely right this time. They would be suited by Olaf Petersen's courses, too, which were certain to be of true Grand Prix proportions. His journey to Dortmund's Grosse Westfallenhalle, the venue for the 12th running of the final, was incident free and far less energy sapping than his trip to Tampa. And, unlike in Tampa, there was no prospect of the horses suffering from the heat. Barring accidents, Milton looked to have the edge on his 45 rivals.

His state of well-being was clearly demonstrated in the way he came bouncing out of his stable on the day before the first leg, eager to get on with the job. He was, as John later confirmed, somewhat over-fresh when he went into the ring for his warm-up competition. He brushed a pole off the fence going into the treble combination and then became so strong round the following turn that his rider had to circle him to get him balanced again. The next morning John put extra work into his partner, to ensure that those exuberant spirits were more in control for the class that mattered.

It became evident that the fates were not entirely on the British pair's side when the draw was announced: Milton's name came out at 14, not a favourable position for the speed class. But John, phlegmatic as ever, was not going to let a bad draw worry him. True, it helps to see where your most dangerous adversaries have saved or wasted time, how difficult lines of fences jump, where strides can be taken out. But an experienced rider, on a horse he knows like the back of his hand, simply goes in and attacks the course. And good performances in the speed competition in Tampa, and again in the European Championships, had given John's confidence a boost.

Olaf Petersen had provided a complex track that at one point invited riders to make navigational errors and which included, for the first time ever in a World Cup

Final, a water jump (as opposed to water ditches, which have been used by Bert de Nemethy and others). The water was a decisive factor, causing 13 horses to fault. No fewer than three of the 13-strong United States contingent made the mistake of swinging round to try and jump it a second time, instead of taking the triple bar next to it. Armand Leone actually did jump it twice and got himself eliminated.

Speaking of Petersen and his course-building techniques, the ever-articulate Ian Millar said

> That man does not have an ounce of mercy in his soul. There was no let-up on the course and if I were a course builder I would never use a water jump where he did, coming off a 180° turn. It teaches horses to land on the tape. But, you have to admit that it got the right horses to the top.

On the way to victory in the Dortmund World Cup Final

Milton snaked round the course with apparent ease, taking the water and the other problems in his stride. Apart from the merest brush of a pole at 12, a big oxer with a 1.70m spread, he did not touch a fence. He was home clear in 69.84 seconds; it looked a satisfactory enough start to the proceedings.

While Milton returned to the comparatively relaxed atmosphere of the stables, John sweated it out at the ringside watching his remaining 32 rivals try, and ultimately fail, to better his time. Afterwards he admitted that doubts had crept into his mind: had he gone fast enough? But, bad draw or not, he knew that there would have been no point in going mad and risking a six-second penalty for a fence down. And in the end his fears were to prove unfounded. Only three other horses were clear and of these the fastest, Jappeloup, was 0.20 of a second slower than Milton. The first goal had been achieved. Milton had won the class and John knew that for him and the grey the worst part was over. The knowledge that the victors of the last three finals had all kicked off by winning the speed leg was a considerable help from a psychological point of view. It was also a great fillip to have European riders occupying the first nine places.

Speaking of the course, John felt it was well judged because it had brought the best half-dozen horses in Europe to the top. 'And it's good,' he added, without the slightest hint of malice, 'to see the Americans behind us.'

With the speed class safely in the bag everyone – John, Tom and Doreen Bradley, Milton's groom Mandy, his adoring fans and not least the nail-biting British journalists – could relax a fraction. The German crowd's appreciation of Milton was nothing short of extraordinary. The friendly Dortmunders, who daily crammed into the 11,000-seat stadium might reasonably have been expected to favour their national heroes Franke Sloothaak and Walzerkönig, who were well in contention after finishing sixth. But much as this powerful pair were appreciated, their reception was nothing compared with that accorded to Milton each time he set hoof into the arena. As the scene was set for the second leg over the usual big Grand Prix course followed by two jump-offs, it was clear exactly who their favourite was and who was going to receive maximum ringside support.

The European domination of this final was underlined on day two when the four United States riders who were among the fourteen to go clear in the initial round all fell by the wayside in the first jump-off. John, surprised that such a big course had produced so many faultless performances, had just one worrying moment in the first round. Realising that he was going a shade too slowly into one of the doubles, he put his leg on to increase the pace but Milton responded by jumping too high at the first element. This in turn caused him to land steeply and rather too short for the second fence. A lesser horse would have found it impossible to stand so far off and still jump the obstacle, but Milton's tremendous scope enabled him to stretch out and clear it, though even he nudged a pole as he did so. Fortunately it remained in its cups. A further clear round in the first jump-off was matched only by the Dutch horse Doreen La Silla, ridden by Jan Tops, the brilliant French speed merchant Norton de Rhuys with Roger-Yves Bost, and Grand Slam, the mount of Nick Skelton.

The mare, Doreen, first to go against the clock, had a fence down but Norton flew round in his inimitable style to throw down a serious challenge to the two British contenders. There are few horses quicker than this French Grand Prix specialist and when he leaves the fences standing he is a truly formidable opponent. Milton, however, had his measure on this occasion, responding with a clear round that was more than a second faster. It looked good enough to enable him to follow in Big Ben's footsteps of a year ago and take the first two legs. But Nick Skelton was in fighting mood, too. He had just lost his sponsor and was also facing the unhappy prospect of having several top horses, including Grand Slam, sold from under him following their owner's decision to pull out of the sport. Not surprisingly he was somewhat off form just before Dortmund, but suddenly, on that Saturday evening, he rode like a man inspired. In steering Grand Slam round clear he reduced the time by another quarter of a second to deprive John and Milton of a £10,000 prize two days running.

This second-leg win pulled Nick up from 14th place into joint fifth. The line-up after the first two days read, John and Milton 0.00, Tops 3.50, Bost 4.00, Michael Whitaker and Mon Santa 5.00, Skelton, and Sloothaak with Walzerkönig, 6.00 each. Pierre Durand and Jappeloup, who had not progressed beyond the first round in the second leg, were nevertheless well placed in seventh on 8.50.

The courses for the second leg had generally met with rider approval. John thought them very good. Ian Millar concurred, saying that most of the distances were 'do-able', though it took quality horses to stand off the planks, with their flat cups, which Olaf Petersen used so many times. However, when it came to the third leg on Easter Monday it was felt that too much was being asked of the horses. The first round, with 13 fences, incorporating 16 jumping efforts, was just about right at that stage. But the second round, with another 12 fences and 15 jumping efforts, was considered too gruelling at the end of a long, hard three days of competition. Franke Sloothaak pointed out that there was no respite for horses between fences and said that two rounds with 31 jumps was excessive. After this final the rules were changed, and a reduction made in the maximum number of obstacles permitted. But those involved in the shake-up in Dortmund simply had to go in and make the best of it.

As in previous years, the points conversion system ensured that the placings at the start of day three were close enough to produce a gripping finale for the crowd. Milton was the only horse to have jumped four clear rounds by that stage, yet he still went into the last leg with an advantage of less than a fence. His cause was considerably helped when the first course produced only four clears besides his own, and none by his closest rivals.

The first came from the experienced United States rider Bernie Traurig. He had been expected to make a good showing with the Dutch gelding Maybe Forever, but finished down the field in the first leg and was eliminated in the second when he inexplicably failed to stop after the bell rang to indicate a refusal. There followed a long sequence of faults before another US rider, Beezie Patton, on Gusty Monroe, jumped a really classic clear round, to be followed By Pierre Durand, Franke Sloothaak and finally John and Milton. Roger-Yves Bost and Jan Tops each collected four faults, which gave John a valuable fence in hand.

Nine riders decided against tackling the controversial second-round course, leaving a field of 25, of whom only six or seven had any realistic chance of claiming a medal. The most influencial obstacle on the course was an offset double, one in which the two fences are not set parallel to each other but on a curve. John was not alone in considering it 'gimmicky', particularly in the confined space of an indoor arena. In the first round it curved to the left and comprised two verticals, the first with a water tray on the take-off side, the second with water on the landing side. Such a combination calls for a totally accurate approach, and 15 out of the 39 survivors from leg two, failed to get it right. Then for the final round Olaf Petersen changed fence A to an oxer over water and the horses were required to jump it on the other rein, that is curving to the right. To add to the difficulties it was now approached from a left-hand turn. A further 12 horses were caught out by it in the second round. Gusty Monroe, unable to manage the distance from the oxer to the vertical, put in such a sudden stop that Beezie Patton was deposited unceremoniously in the water tray.

The first of those to go still in with any chance was John's brother. But Mon Santa, with two fences down in round one, was in difficulty at the treble in the early part of the course. He hit the first two parts, frightened himself and ground to a halt at the third. Michael ended up on the floor and decided to call it a day. Grand Slam began to find things beyond him, too. He made three mistakes, which left Nick Skelton unable to improve on his overall sixth place. Jappeloup, on the other hand, was in great spirits. He made just the one error, at the the first part of the curved double, for a three-day total of 12.50. When Norton de Rhuys faulted twice and Doreen La Silla three times, Pierre Durand suddenly found himself in third position.

The tension in Dortmund's Westfalenhalle was all but tangible as the last two protagonists prepared to tackle the course. Europe was already assured of victory. But could Germany's Olympic pair hold on to second place and put pressure on Milton by jumping a clear round? With a track this size no one could afford to relax until the last fence was safely negotiated. Walzerkönig had put his supporters' hearts in their mouths during the first round when he rattled two early fences before settling to his job. This time, alas, the poles simply refused to stay up. A groan went up from the stands as the second part of the treble, fence three, fell. Now he had only 2.50 faults to spare over Jappeloup. The next seven fences were negotiated successfully, but the

German horse, like Jappeloup, failed to clear part one of the double and Franke dropped to third place behind his French rival.

Now, for the first time in his long riding career, John Whitaker came into the arena for the last round with the World Cup within his grasp. The only person to have competed in every final, he had never been this close before. A deathly hush settled over the huge crowd. There was surely no one present who did not want the grey horse to win. Stifled gasps accompanied his faultless progress over the first ten fences. Then John turned him to the dreaded double of water ditches. His approach looked perfect but to those watching in the stands Milton appeared to try to jump too big. He caught the back rail of the oxer and as it tumbled to the ground, accompanied by another great groan from the audience, he seemed to stop in surprise, caught off balance and searching for his stride to the second element. It was a moment when his boundless scope, his courage and his athleticism were all called into play and it was a tribute to him and his cool-headed rider that he managed to gather himself up to clear the vertical. The final oxer was almost easy by comparison. As he touched down safely, 11,000 voices erupted in greeting to the first European World Cup winner since 1979.

John, looking more pale than usual, came through the finish shaking his head. He knew he had won, but his elation was tinged with disappointment for Milton. The horse had tried so hard, he had jumped 75 fences without incurring one mistake, and John felt he did not deserve to have a fence down so close to home.

> He was jumping fantastically, but he was tending to back off because the fences were so big and I was probably having to push a bit more than normal. The first part of the double was very big and he tried to over-jump it. When he caught the back bar it stopped him in his tracks. It wasn't tiredness, it's just that when you keep asking horses to jump big fences they get a little frightened and that makes them try to jump too big. Two rounds of 13 and 12 fences for the third leg was really asking too much.

Only two horses had jumped the last track without error, the luckless Maybe Forever, whose spirited finish pulled him up to eighth place overall, and the remarkable Ian Millar's new partner, Czar. The Canadian's confident performance with the latter provided an object lesson in polished horsemanship and the pair deserved to finish in the money in 12th place.

John's disappointment was soon forgotten as Milton led the way in for the awards ceremony, closely attended by Jappeloup, runner-up for the second time in three years, and Walzerkönig. European horses and riders filled the first six places.

It had taken ten years for Europe to lay the ghost of the World Cup. It had taken Milton, champion of Europe, to do it.

CHAPTER 13

TAKING ON THE WORLD

Milton's domination of the Dortmund World Cup Final fuelled hopes for yet more success later that year. Having resisted the temptation to tackle the 1986 World Championships with him during his first full international season, John could look ahead to the 1990 World Equestrian Games, scheduled to take place in Stockholm during the summer, safe in the knowledge that the mature Milton was well up to the challenge. Not since David Broome's victory 20 years earlier had the World title come to Britain. What better combination to bid for an individual medal than John and Milton – especially in a year which promised to be so memorable for equestrian sport as a whole.

For the first time the world championships in all six disciplines (show jumping, three-day eventing, dressage, carriage driving, endurance riding and vaulting), customarily staged every four years in six different locations, were being brought together to form one gigantic equestrian tournament. It would be the biggest horse show the world had seen. Older members of the horse world harboured fond memories of the Swedish capital, which had hosted the equestrian disciplines of the 1956 Olympics when quarantine restrictions prevented their being held in Melbourne. Many people still considered them the best equestrian games ever staged. Now, in 1990, at this showcase for equestrian events, Britain would be wielding the most powerful show jumping weapon it had ever had in its armoury.

Refreshed after a six-week holiday following his World Cup success, Milton was given two pipe-openers, the first at the Oldcotes Charity Show, the second at the Royal Bath and West, before joining the British team at Hickstead at the end of May in preparation for the build-up to this second major objective of the season.

Unusually the British public was able to see their champion at four consecutive shows: he finished runner-up in the Area International Trial at Oldcotes, runner-up in the big class at the Royal Bath and West, and runner-up in the £60,000 Emirates Airline Cup (the British Grand Prix) at Hickstead. Favourite to win the latter event, he looked to have things sewn up with a tremendously fast clear round in a high-class jump-off. But another Hickstead specialist had the benefit of the last draw: Apollo. On the perfect grass surface, which always brought out his best, Apollo responded to a typically dashing piece of riding by Nick Skelton to trim nearly a second off the World Cup winners' time. Two days later, though, Milton showed his true colours by jumping a double-clear round in the Nations Cup for the third year running. His performance ensured that Britain finished the two rounds on level terms with one of the strongest Irish contingents ever to visit the Sussex show ground. Eddie Macken and his mare, Welfenkrone, were the only pair, other than John and the grey, to finish without faults and for a few minutes it looked as if he and his team-mates might record their first Nations Cup win on British soil for 53 years. Always welcome visitors to British shows, they put up a gallant fight but were finally forced to concede defeat in the jump-off. By the time the third horses had jumped, a British victory was assured and Milton was not required to come out again.

A win on home soil is always a good morale booster, particularly when you have not enjoyed one for five years. This time, however, elation was tempered slightly by the necessity of going to a jump-off. Team manager Ronnie Massarella, anxious to

DELIGHTED TEAM MANAGER RONNIE MASSARELLA WITH THE EDWARD, PRINCE OF WALES CUP AFTER A BRITISH VICTORY IN THE HICKSTEAD TEAM CONTESTIN 1990. JOHN'S TEAM-MATES ARE (FROM LEFT) HIS BROTHER MICHAEL, DAVID BROOME AND EMMA-JANE MAC

conserve his horses' energies in the run-up to the Games, would have preferred it to have been otherwise. But Milton, at least, had been spared the necessity of jumping a third round.

Not wishing to overtax him so close to the Championships, John gave him a two-week break before the Royal International in the middle of June where his prime target was the elusive King George V Gold Cup. On his first appearance on the opening night Milton was narrowly beaten on time by My Mesieur, a horse formerly ridden by Malcolm Pyrah, now the mount of John's brother Michael. But 48 hours later Milton thrilled his rider and the Bradleys, not to mention the crowd, by finally capturing the show's most prestigious trophy. Third in 1987, runner-up in 1988 and 1989, Milton had, John felt, been unlucky not to win the King's Cup before. This time he was not to be denied. He was the only contender in the five-horse jump-off to complete a third clear round.

Afterwards John credited his wife, Clare, with giving him a valuable piece of advice as he entered the arena: take care at the wall. For spectators viewing from the stands, it is all too easy to forget that a competitor preparing his horse to come in for a jump-off has no time to see how the course is riding. At such a time it is of inestimable value to have someone on the ground feeding you with information. On this occasion Clare had seen the first two horses fault at the big wall, fence two, and her advice to be especially careful was well founded. John let Milton take his time at that particular obstacle and it paid off.

The day was an especially satisfying one for Doreen and Tom Bradley. Earlier the women's equivalent of the King George, the Queen Elizabeth II Cup, had been won by a former pupil of Caroline's, Emma-Jane Mac. Caroline, of course, had won it twice, on the first occasion with Milton's sire, Marius.

On the closing night in Birmingham Belgium's Ludo Philippaerts and Fidelgo, runners-up with the fastest four faults for the King's Cup, took their revenge in the Grand Prix. John and Milton were clear and fast in the jump-off, but Ludo made full use of his late draw, clipping more than half-a-second off Milton's time. However, it had been a more than satisfactory week, and Milton's name was now engraved on yet another of the sport's most prestigious trophies.

In the weeks between Birmingham and the World Games, John jumped him in three hand-picked shows on the Continent, Franconville, Zurich and Luxembourg. The level of prize-money at events such as these explains just why leading riders spend so much of their time away from home. One win and three placings earned Milton £23,000. Indeed, for finishing fifth in the Euro Classic at Zurich, he took home more prize-money than for winning the King's Cup.

It takes a special kind of skill to produce a horse to peak condition month after month, year after year. John's mastery of the art can be compared with that of the finest racehorse trainers, who bring their top performers to peak just when it matters most. With a horse like Milton the temptation must always be present to jump him one more time, to try for one more prize purse. But the policy with Milton has been to bring him out at most three times, often only twice, at the majority of shows, and the success of this policy speaks for itself.

As the World Games approached the most important thing was that Milton was jumping clear round after clear round with relentless precision. He was clearly still enjoying himself and he arrived in Stockholm fit and ready to take on the world.

Sadly, storm clouds gathered over the whole sport of show jumping in the run-up to the Games following the publication in *Stern* Magazine of cruelty allegations aimed at, among others, Paul Schockemöhle's establishment, which would be fielding half of the German team. Sweden has particularly stringent animal protection laws and rumour was rife that disruptive protests would be made during the actual Games. Fortunately, these did not materialise and the Games were a resounding success from a sporting, if not a financial, point of view.

Whatever had or had not been perpetrated during training, once the horses arrived in Stockholm every effort was made to ensure that they were not 'got at' during the Games. International Equestrian Federation stewards were conspicuous at all exercise and practice areas, and the new yellow-card warning system, introduced by the Federation earlier in the year to give them the power to take action against anyone infringing the rules at international events, was brought into effect. Testifying to the vigilance of the stewarding, three yellow cards were issued in Stockholm, one, significantly, to an American jumping rider for the misuse of spurs.

Once the jumping programme started and it became evident that there would be no riotous behaviour in the stands, even when Schockemöhle's riders Otto Becker and Rene Tebbel appeared, riders and public alike settled back to enjoy four days of tremendous competition.

The venue for the jumping championships was the historic stadium originally built for the 1912 Olympics, used for the 1956 equestrian events and nowadays normally a football stadium. For the 1990 Games four million pounds had been spent on renovations and improvements, among them a green Fibresand surface. Olaf Petersen, brought in to design the courses, followed up his success in Seoul by again taking local themes as the inspiration for some strikingly handsome obstacles.

Britain's riders, hoping to take home at least one gold medal, had to settle for a silver and a bronze. Ironically, it was Milton's tremendous popularity which deprived his country of the team silver.

The speed competition on the first day was won, somewhat surprisingly, by the Spaniard Cayetano Martinez de Irujo on Winston Elegast, who was clear and nearly three seconds faster than runner-up Roger-Yves Bost with Norton de Rhuys. Cayetano, who comes from Madrid but had been trained in Holland by Henk Nooren, was as amazed as anyone to find himself in that position and was perhaps not altogether surprised when he began to slide down the order on the second day.

From a field of 75 only eight horses recorded clear rounds. Milton was not among them, having brushed a rail off the 11th, an oxer built as a Viking boat. However, despite a seven-second penalty, his total time was still good enough to put him in a handy ninth place. None of his team-mates managed to go clear, either, and Britain was lying only sixth at the end of the day. The leaders, France, had a clear one-fence advantage, but the next five nations were within a point or two of each other and Ronnie Massarella felt confident that his 'boys' would catch up over the bigger fences in the Nations Cup.

Michael Whitaker helped to boost British hopes of pegging back the French with a magnificent first clear round in the team final with Mon Santa. Over these bigger fences which Milton relishes so much, John was naturally expected to emulate his brother. But for once Milton's supporters did him a disservice. He is a horse who is acutely aware of everything going on around him – John recalls times when he has been distracted in the ring merely because somebody standing in a corner has moved.

John is not a rider who looks for excuses but even he admits that on this occasion Milton's concentration was severely affected, first by the crowd and then, by the photographers. All went well over the first eight fences. Then as Milton safely negotiated the big treble combination at nine, situated alongside the grandstand, the crowd let out a cheer of approval. At the same time a clutch of photographers, ranged alongside on the athletics track, began running *en masse* to take up new positions. As John swung Milton to the right to approach a tricky narrow white gate, the horse's attention, already slightly disturbed by the crowd, was clearly not on the fence ahead but on the photographers and it must be remembered that because of the way a horse's eyes are positioned he has an enormous field of vision to the rear. As John explained:

> They were just behind him and that made it worse because he was looking back at them while I was trying to make him look at the fence. When we did reach it he was only half looking at it and he went straight through it. Normally if he does have a fence, it is because he has just touched the top. But he would have had that one down if it had been only 3ft high. I don't like looking for excuses, but it was definitely distracting.

It was a tremendous disappointment, particularly when Milton was evidently in such fine form. He jumped a splendid clear on his second appearance. So, too, did Mon Santa, except for a fraction of a time fault. But the Whitakers' team-mates, Nick Skelton on Grand Slam and David Broome on Lannegan, collected faults in both rounds, and although the quartet went well enough overall to pull up three places, Britain lost the silver to the Germans by 1.35 faults.

The one consolation was that Milton had edged up into sixth place individually (without that fence down he would have been second). In the lead was one of the triumphant French team, Eric Navet and his young home-bred stallion Quito de Baussy, closely followed by Greg Best with Gem Twist, and Belgium's Ludo Philippaerts with another stallion, Darco. All three of the leading horses had jumped double-clear rounds in the Nations Cup. In fourth and fifth places were Otto Becker on Paul Schockemöhle's mare Pamina and Michael Whitaker with Mon Santa. Ranging up in seventh and eighth, and underlining the strength of the French squad, were Hubert Bourdy on Morgat and the Olympic champions, Pierre Durand and Jappeloup.

The team championship was followed by a rest day before the top 20 riders went into the third competition, a two-rounder, to decide the four who would go forward to the change-horse individual final, the last event of the Games. As in other championships, the scores from the speed competition, the Nations Cup and the Grand Prix-type class were cumulative.

By the end of the first round John had moved up into fourth place. With no distractions this time from the photographers, Milton jumped a superb clear round over Olaf Petersen's testing 12-fence track and although John incurred half-a-time fault, his score was good enough to take him within firing range of his first final.

Eric Navet, the overnight leader, slipped to third after the relatively inexperienced Quito de Baussy rattled both parts of the double at the fourth and then lowered a rail at the 11th. He was overtaken by Greg Best and Ludo Philippaerts, who both recorded clear rounds. Michael Whitaker's chances of joining his brother in the final evaporated when Mon Santa made two mistakes and slipped to eighth place. Pierre Durand pulled Jappeloup out after round one, in which he made three mistakes. The horse was thought to be suffering from colic though happily he made a quick recovery.

Over the second course, Greg Best completed the only totally double clear of the competition to maintain his lead, while Eric Navet, clear except for a time fault, edged back up into second. John, going ultra carefully to ensure that Milton cleared the fences, was again outside the time, but his otherwise faultless performance took him into second place in the class and third overall, which assured him of that much coveted place in the final. The fourth man to qualify was Hubert Bourdy. His two-round total of 4.50 was sufficient to take him more than two faults ahead of the luckless Ludo Philippaerts, who had a disastrous round on Darco to finish with 12.25.

At the end of the three strenuous legs, the scoreboard read: Greg Best and Gem Twist (USA) 4.38; Eric Navet and Quito de Baussy (France) 8.92; John Whitaker and Milton (GB) 9.30 and Hubert Bourdy and Morgat (France) 14.08. France was the first country to have two riders in the final since Britain back in 1970, when David Broome won and Harvey Smith took the bronze.

Sunday, August 5, dawned dry and sunny. It was John's 35th birthday and hopes were high in the British camp that he would take home the best-ever anniversary gift: the World title. Although he is not particularly in favour of the format of the final, the prospect of strangers riding his horse did not worry him. 'I was quite looking forward to it in some ways,' he recalled:

> I suppose there's always that element of doubt when someone else is riding your horse, but at least you know that at the World Championships they are going to be quite good riders. Milton certainly didn't feel any different afterwards.

Because the riders are required to jump strange horses, the course for the final is always smaller and more straightforward than that for the preceding rounds of the championship. The eight fences in Stockholm included just one combination, a treble, at seven. In round one the riders all starting on zero scores jump their own horses, switching in succeeding rounds to those of their rivals. Each rider has only three minutes in which to warm up their next horse, not long to become accustomed to a strange partner. This warming-up process takes place in a fenced-off part of the main arena, so the whole contest provides a fascinating spectacle for the crowd.

Eric Navet, with the number one draw, finished on four faults with his own

GIVING AN OXER PLENTY
OF DAYLIGHT IN THE
WORLD GAMES

horse, Quito de Baussy, who lowered the final element of the treble. Greg Best and Gem Twist finished on the same score after taking a rail off the oxer at four. Milton next to go, touched the same fence behind but was home without faults, as were Hubert Bourdy and Morgat.

By the end of round two, however, the placings had been shuffled into what was virtually the overall finishing order. Eric produced a clear round from the American horse to go into the lead. John slipped to second after collecting eight faults on Morgat, the horse he had thought would suit him best. Greg, failing to find the key to Milton, also had two fences down to share third place with Hubert, who had three fences down with Quito de Baussy.

In round three, Milton went much better for Eric than he had for Greg. The Frenchman was able to consolidate his position by completing another clear round, except for half a time fault. By now the die was cast, and the four faults which John scored with Eric's horse at the middle of the treble ultimately had no effect on the overall placings. One fence down for Hubert, on Gem Twist, as opposed to two for Greg on Morgat, took the second Frenchman into the bronze medal position, which is where he stayed.

Eric Navet went into the final round with a fence in hand over John and when Morgat jumped clear for him it clinched the title. Greg had a rather dramatic four faults at the sixth fence with Quito de Baussy, who hit a pole of this oxer behind, bouncing it up into the air. It returned momentarily to its cups, only to bounce out again. Had it stayed put, he would have jumped off for the bronze with Hubert, who also had four faults on his last ride – Milton.

John's final appearance was with Gem Twist, and how well the other grey went for him – such a different performer from his own. 'He felt brilliant. He's really quick off the floor, totally different from Milton. In some ways he would suit my style of riding even better than Milton.' Indeed, Gem Twist came up so fast at the treble that he took John by surprise, hitting him in the face and cutting his lip in the process.

As he wiped the blood from his face and prepared for the awards ceremony, John was pleased enough to have finished second. He had always known that it would be something of a lottery. The order in which the riders are drawn inevitably affects the performance of the horses. One rider is bound to get on with a particular horse better than another, one will unsettle a horse more than another.

John felt that, of his three rivals, Eric Navet got the best tune out of Milton.

But he also had the benefit of Greg Best having ridden him beforehand. Greg thought he was going to take him into his fences as he does Gem Twist. But even though Milton has a lot of scope and looks as if he's jumping things very easily, he just needs a little bit of pushing. He hit the middle part of the treble quite hard and Navet got the benefit of that.

The horses were all very different to ride. Quito de Baussy felt better than I expected. I think that sometimes he looks a bit stuffy and stalliony and as if he's jumping rather resentfully, but he felt quite good. Morgat was what I expected. I felt beforehand that I would manage him better than the other riders because he's quite small and quick and I seem to get on well with that sort. The double I had down was really my fault. I had seen him tip up over exactly the same combination in Zurich earlier in the year and I just overrode him. I saw a stride and pushed him into it instead of waiting and trusting him to jump it. Everyone tries to get on a horse and ride it in the same way as its own rider, but once you start your round and you've jumped two or three fences, you revert back to your own style.

This was where Greg Best came unstuck with Milton. The American's horse tends to run on at his fences and generally does things his way, whereas the super-obedient Milton expects to be organised more by the chap on top.

The Bradleys, like John, had expected the two French riders to provide the biggest threat. Doreen said she was not surprised when Eric Navet won, 'because like John he is a good rider of many horses and rode them all sympathetically. I have always liked Hubert Bourdy's riding, too, though he has not had such good horses.' Some people expressed surprise when Milton's owners readily agreed to his going to Stockholm but not the Olympics. But Stockholm, Doreen Bradley reasoned, was not expected 'to take the top off horses' as the Olympics can, and like John she had no doubt that only good riders would reach the final.

When all is said and done, however, there is no doubt that the format of the individual World Championship leaves much to be desired. John, in common with most other riders, would like to see the change-horse final changed:

Even though I really enjoyed taking part and it's very interesting for the public, I don't think it's the real way to decide the World Championships because so often it's not the true champion horse/rider combination that wins. In Stockholm Greg Best and Gem Twist were the best of the four qualifiers, but finished only fourth. The same thing happened in Aachen to Pierre Durand and Jappeloup. In fact, usually the rider with the best horse seems to have the worst chance when he gets into the final. It would be better to decide it on the three legs, like in the Europeans, and then perhaps have a change-horse contest to decide the champion horseman.

In Aachen, Pierre Durand's rivals had nominated Jappeloup as their favourite horse, after their own. In Stockholm, it came as no surprise to hear Milton receiving the popularity vote. Eric Navet said, 'I preferred Milton by far. He is so well trained and has such a good temperament.' Hubert Bourdy agreed, saying that he was the best horse in the field. Greg Best, who had not the opportunity to assess Milton in action as frequently as his European rivals, admitted that he hadn't ridden him aggressively enough. He summed up his meeting with the European Champion by adding: 'It's like having a date with the most beautiful woman in the world. You trip over your feet a few times.'

At the beginning of September the British team had the satisfaction of turning the tables on the entire French gold medal-winning squad from Stockholm in the Calgary Nations Cup. John Whitaker, his brother Michael and Nick Skelton were joined by Emma-Jane Mac on Oyster (replacing David Broome and Lannegan) and emerged the victors, after a tough contest, by 24 faults to France's 28. Milton jumped a clear first round and was not required to start a second time.

The European Champion, World Cup holder and World Equestrian Games silver medallist was greeted ecstatically when he returned to the Horse of the Year Show the following month. Friday night's performance was sold out in expectation of another devastating display by the grey superstar in the International Masters, but, incredibly, the favourite failed to qualify for the week's top prize.

The first of the three qualifying competitions was the Pedigree Chum Classic, a jump-off class, on the second night of the show. Milton needed to finish in the top two to be assured of his place in the Masters. To begin with everything went smoothly and he jumped a good clear in the first round. Then in the jump-off, his fans were left open mouthed with astonishment as they witnessed something that was virtually unheard of: Milton actually stopped at a fence. After hitting the first obstacle, he lost his impulsion and ground to a halt at the second. He finished 12th.

The explanation, fortunately, was a simple one and had nothing to do with the horse either feeling unwell or lacking enthusiasm for his work. John said that Milton's concentration had suddenly lapsed and he blamed himself for giving his partner too little work between Calgary and Wembley. As far as anyone could remember it was only the second time that Milton had stopped in a competition. The first was in Bordeaux a couple of years earlier, but that had been more a case of John pulling him off a fence when he realised that his approach was wrong. There were two more chances for Milton to qualify for the Masters, though because one was a speed competition – something in which John would not normally jump him – niggling doubts began to creep in.

John had to make a quick change of plan. Instead of starting Milton in the Leading Show Jumper of the Year on the Wednesday night, he switched to Grannusch, re-routing Milton to the following day's Modern Alarms Cup, where once again the top two qualified for the Masters. Once more he went through to the jump-off with no problem, and with the luck of the draw on his side – last but one of the 16 clears – he looked to have a reasonably good chance of success. But it was not to be. Fast and clear though he was, he could finish only third behind Michael and Mon Santa and

Janet Hunter and Lisnamarrow.

That really set the alarm bells ringing. John had no alternative but to run Milton in the speed class on the Friday afternoon, hardly his greatest forte. The talented young Nigel Coupe on Invincible Lad took an early lead, then was overtaken by his great rival Marie Edgar with her versatile, Young Riders European Champion Surething. Milton clocked up the third fastest time and for a while looked home and dry. However, Otto Becker, with the third-last draw on Paul Schockemöhle's impressive horse Richard, overtook Nigel Coupe to snatch second place. Once more John found himself out-pointed by a fraction of a second.

Just as everyone was regretfully getting used to the idea that the Masters would start without its chief attraction, there came the surprise announcement that Nigel had decided to pull out. The instant and understandable outside reaction was that pressure had been put upon him to do so, but he denied this. He had put the 15-year-old Invincible Lad in the speed competition more because it was a good class for his horse than with any ambition to qualify for the Masters. He, his father and apparently his trainer Michael Whitaker, all felt that a possible five-round contest over big fences might be too severe a test for Invincible Lad and that a horse of his advancing years would be better saved for the Grand Prix. Nigel's withdrawal conveniently let in the next best placed horse – Milton. Though evidently disappointed, Nigel, one of the sport's best ambassadors from the younger generation, stoically added 'The crowd would rather see Milton than me anyway.' And who, in all conscience, could disagree with him?

After such a controversial lead-up to the big competition, there was even more pressure on John and Milton to go well. And of course Milton, seeming as usual to sense the importance of the occasion, rose to the challenge. His number-four draw was not ideal but by systematically increasing the height and spread of the oxers, John effectively outwitted the opposition. Starting in second place in the fifth and final round, he took up the option of raising not one but two fences. Milton, very much in his element, cleared the entire course in impressive fashion, leaving his rider to stand back and watch his two remaining rivals, Janet Hunter and Otto Becker, try to deprive him of a remarkable hat-trick. Neither succeeded. A fence down apiece by these two left the European Champions with a record first prize of £29,000. The following night, they just failed to better the time set by Nick Skelton and Grand Slam in the Grand Prix, but earned enough to take their four-day total to £35,400.

Milton was given a short holiday before John took him on his customary annual visit to Stuttgart. There he was given his usual rapturous welcome and his numerous fans were excited at the prospect of seeing him try to win his third Mercedes-Benz Jumping Masters in a row. He duly beat Otto Becker and his Calgary Grand Prix winner Pamina to take the first Masters qualifier, which assured him of a place among the thirteen to start for the big prize. This select field included the new World

FENCE DESIGNING HAS REACHED NEW ARTISTIC HEIGHTS DURING THE LAST FEW YEARS. HERE JOHN AND MILTON ARE FRAMED BY TREES, FLOWERS AND BUTTERFLIES ON A SUNNY DAY IN STOCKHOLM

Champions and Germany's Olympic bronze medallists Karsten Huck and Nepomuk.

No Mercedes came his way, though. It was one of those days when the clock in John's head let him down. In the first round Milton, in superb form, finished without jumping faults but was just outside the time. He missed going through to the jump-off for the car by a quarter of a fault.

John, the Bradleys and his enthusiastic supporters in the crowd hoped for better things in the Grand Prix in which Milton looked very impressive as he jumped a double clear to join five others in the jump-off for the £6,000 first prize. If any of the photographers could have foreseen what would happen next, he or she would

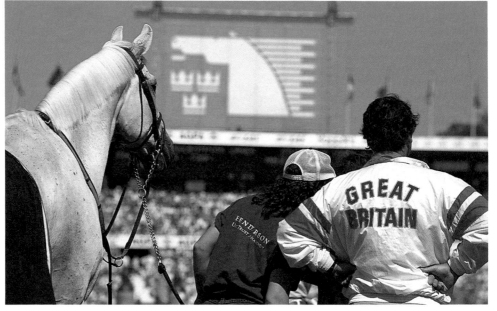

Milton keeping a close eye on the progress of his rivals in the World Individual Final in Stockholm

have made a small fortune overnight. The incident, sadly, seems to have remained unrecorded for posterity.

At one end of the arena was a group of three fences, radiating out from the same central point like the spokes of a wheel. One was fence three, one was eight and the other ten. The approach to ten came after a left-hand turn. Having landed over ten, the horses were then required to sweep round to the right to the last fence. This complex called for the usual sort of accurate, controlled riding associated with jump-offs for major Grand Prix competitions. Yet it turned out to be one of the very few occasions when John and Milton failed to understand each other. John executed a particularly tight turn to fence ten. Milton rather twisted over it which slightly unbalanced John, who was already preparing for his right-hand turn. Perhaps surprised at finding his jockey out of his usual secure seat, and perhaps remembering that in the two previous rounds he had been asked to turn left after jumping this fence, Milton dodged to the left as he landed. John, alas, didn't. The result was a celebrated parting

SHOWING A CLEAN PAIR OF HEELS DURING THE WORLD EQUESTRIAN GAMES IN STOCKHOLM'S historic 1912 OLYMPIC STADIUM

of the ways – their first in public in five seasons at top-level competition.

As John descended to the ground Milton, pulling himself up at the boards, turned to regard his partner, a quizzical expression on his face as if wondering where he had gone. The crowd, momentarily stunned, collapsed with merriment. Reunited, the pair completed the course to finish sixth. At the prize giving John was presented with a bottle of champagne. He did not know why. 'Entertainment value, perhaps,' he grinned. Win or lose, Milton could not avoid being the star of the show.

It was during this show that one of the Stuttgart organisers, Hans-Peter Bauer, was presented with an unusual Milton memento in celebration of his 44th birthday. The gift, organised by the press office, comprised a lock of hair from Milton's famous white tail. Penny was commissioned to provide it – 'he almost kicked me out of the box,' she admitted, as she handed over the prized trophy to the British journalists deputed to act as go betweens.

Shortly afterwards Milton's 1990 season ground to a premature halt. Having travelled on to Vienna, where he was third in the Grand Prix, and then to Maastricht, he should have proceeded to Hanover and Frankfurt. But in Hanover he went off his food and for a horse who lists eating as his number-one interest in life that is a serious sign. He was found to be running a slight temperature and was immediately sent home. A respiratory virus was diagnosed, and although he recovered fairly quickly, John felt that there was too little time to get him fit for Olympia. It was the first time in his international career that illness or lameness had prevented him from competing – a remarkable record for a show jumper.

Despite this early close to his year, he finished 1990 with winnings of £182,737 against his name, more than three times the amount won by his nearest rival, Phoenix Park. It took his career total to more than £700,000.

CHAPTER 14

BEHIND THE SCENES

When Milton goes home to John's Yorkshire stables for a holiday he is not, as might be imagined, let down completely. Years ago, when show jumping was an April-to-October sport, horses were often taken out of work altogether during the winter months. Then there was time to bring them back gradually to fitness. Nowadays, with the proliferation of indoor shows, jumping is virtually a year-round activity. Only January and February are more or less blank months, and even these are steadily being encroached upon as shows find it more and more difficult to secure a slot in the crowded calendar.

Milton, like most other international horses, needs to peak several times annually. There is the World Cup Final in April then, depending on the year, the European or World Championships in the summer. As autumn sets in there is a new round of big indoor Grand Prix competitions and World Cup qualifiers to aim for. He is, accordingly, given several short holidays each year rather than one long one. With this system riders find it easier to keep horses fit, particularly as they get older. And besides, turning Milton out to grass for long periods would not be viable because being by nature a greedy fellow he would quickly become too fat.

During his rest periods he is turned out in his paddock – one without too much rich grass – for at least part of the day, depending on the weather, and goes back in his stable at night. Turning valuable competition animals out always involves an element of risk. Horses are notoriously adept at getting themselves into trouble, even in an apparently safe field, and there is always the chance that they might kick each other. John, like many other riders, has separate, adjacent paddocks in which his jumpers can be turned out alone, though within sight of each other so that they do not feel lonely or become bored.

Hillwork is the best way of getting and keeping horses fit and John is lucky to live in an area where hacking out on the roads and moors, plus the odd gallop, is all that is needed to keep a horse ticking over between shows. Nevertheless exercising Milton is not always the most pleasurable activity. Because he is so spooky only John and Tracey Newman, his stable jockey, ever ride him out and even Tracey will retreat to the safety of the covered school if it is particularly windy.

As Ron Longford discovered all those years ago when Milton was recovering from his split tendon operation, he is the sort of horse who will pass a lorry on the road without a problem, then nearly turn a somersault at the sight of a piece of paper in the hedge. The worry is always that he might eject his rider and gallop off loose or injure himself when he finally does come down to earth. John says that he will still spook at the same thing day after day, even though he knows it is there, has seen it many times before and must realise that it is not going to harm him.

He'll spook at something and fall into a ditch he hasn't noticed, or run into something twice as dangerous as the thing he's spooked at. It only takes a bird to fly out from behind a wall and you'll find yourself on the other side of the road. People always say that brilliant horses tend to be more intelligent, but I sometimes think that Milton is a bit thick!

Perhaps he is just a bit whimsical.

One thing, though, that has never been a problem, is maintaining his athletic ability. He is given hardly any jumping at home, just a short school or two after a holiday before going to his first show. Milton is not a horse who needs hours and hours of training to get him into the right outline. John has no more to teach him

about technique and provided he is tuned up and supple it is pointless to keep testing his jumping prowess outside the arena.

There is, anyway, no substitute for competition. As John says, 'No matter how fit you think you've got horses at home, you take them to a show and they come out blowing.' Often, however, he finds that one local outing is sufficient for Milton after a rest. If he goes well, John will take him straight off abroad.

Once he arrives at a show, John usually gives him half an hour's work each day. 'Sometimes if he's not jumping, I might take him out twice, once in the morning, once in the evening, just to break the day up for him. Normally I don't do much jumping. It depends how he feels. With Milton you can give him two weeks off and take him to a show and he'll jump better for it, whereas some horses would need quite a bit of work and getting ready. Up to a point, the fresher Milton is the better.'

An international show jumper's life is rather like that of a touring actor, moving on every few days to a new venue. The riders can often fly home between shows, but it would be too expensive to do that with the horses and it would take too long to box them back, so they tend to go from show to show, making overnight stops where necessary. The stables belonging to German rider Peter Weinberg and his English-born wife Helena, situated near Aachen, are a favourite stopping-off spot for British horses. The Weinbergs have a separate 'visitors' yard' to house the peripatetic animals of their fellow competitors. John uses this establishment a lot: 'You can get to pretty well any of the continental shows in reasonable time from Aachen.'

Penny Stevens, Milton's groom and constant companion for the last few years, travels with him on these occasions. When she first had him in her care she would not risk riding him, but now in between shows, when John is not there, she does

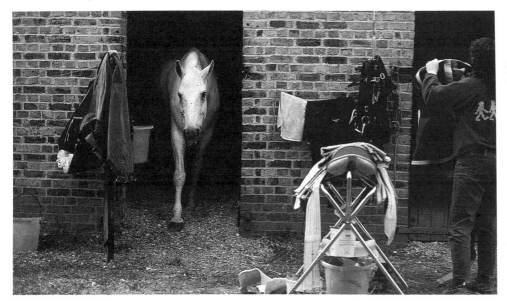

MILTON SPOTS A CHANCE TO GO WALKABOUTS. HE IS SO INQUISITIVE THAT HE IS ALWAYS LOOKING FOR OPPORTUNITIES TO ESCAPE FROM HIS STABLE

exercise him – provided there is somewhere she can control him safely. There are, though, still many places where it is safer to lead him about than to try riding him. His phobias include a dislike of hose-pipes and wire, so that getting him from A to B at showgrounds where there are television cables trailing everywhere can be a headache. There is always the danger that he might spook and injure not only himself but also members of the public.

He has never overcome his dislike of the clippers or of hypodermic syringes, either. Steve Hadley remembers how as a young horse Milton would take one look at a syringe and leap, not as might be expected, away from it but towards the person wielding it. He stills does so, making life especially difficult for the vets required to take routine dope tests at shows.

Fortunately for a horse required to cover tens of thousands of miles every year,

MILTON WITH MANDY THOMAS, HIS GROOM WHEN HE FIRST JOINED JOHN WHITAKER'S STABLE. A COMPETENT, CARING GROOM IS A VITAL COMPONENT OF ANY SHOW JUMPING OPERATION

he is not particularly worried by travelling. 'On the whole he's a good traveller,' says John, 'though he does tend to fidget. He gets bored easily and will try to bite or kick the other horses in the box.' Apart from one particularly rough crossing back from Gothenburg he has not been upset by sea travel and mercifully he has never panicked while in a plane, unlike the nervous French mare Punition who gave everyone a nasty scare five hours into the flight to the 1992 World Cup Final in Del Mar. She began thrashing about so violently in her stall that it registered on the cockpit instruments. Under these circumstances there is no alternative but to give the horse a sedative – which is all very well if the horse does not, like Milton, have an aversion to needles.

Milton's fairly laid-back attitude to travel has stood him in good stead during his busy international career. Horses who are difficult to load and are inclined to fret in transit all too often leave their best performance on the road. The demands made on these equine athletes are considerable and can be appreciated by taking a look at a typical journey undertaken by British horses, who have the added problem of a sea voyage every time they compete in Europe.

The lorry carrying Milton and John's other mounts leaves Yorkshire at midday, stopping over at Joe Turi's yard in Warwickshire to pick up. From there the journey takes them to the quarantine stables a mile outside Dover. For the crossing to the Continent by drive-on, drive-off ferry, the horses are again loaded in the box. On the other side of the channel they are either driven direct to the show or, if that is too far to accomplish in one day, they might stay overnight at the Weinbergs', completing the journey the following day. Normally the longest period they are asked to travel in one day is six hours, but always there is the danger of a hold-up for customs. Even today, when border crossings are as a general rule much more straightforward than in the past, it is still not unknown for horses to be kept standing in the lorry for hours on end while the paperwork is sorted out.

Long-distance flying, too, is just as stressful for horses as it is for humans – more so, in fact, since they cannot leave their stalls and walk about when they feel stiff. The horses who are loaded first have the worst time since they may be required to stand there for several hours before the plane is even ready to take off. No wonder Milton, normally the best of loaders, takes a bit of encouragement to go up the narrow ramps on to aircraft.

Once he is installed at a show, Milton quickly settles in even though the stabling is often cramped and uncomfortable compared with his roomy box at home. However, his curiosity is as insatiable as ever and he has never overcome his overriding desire to get out of his stable whenever possible and take a look around outside.

Removing his rugs and bandages is his other incurable habit, a trait he inherited from his father. The one thing to be said in Milton's favour is that he at least takes his rugs off in one piece. Marius used to tear his off in strips.

CHAPTER 15

THE TOUGHEST COMBINATION IN THE WORLD

Waiting in the tunnel to go into the arena in Gothenburg, John and Milton must have at least a glimmering of an idea of how it felt to be a favourite gladiator in ancient Rome. The clapping, cheering and stamping feet of 11,000 fans, amplified to ear-splitting proportions in the narrow chute, create an awesome wall of sound through which horse and rider must pass when their turn comes to jump. No need for the announcer to tell this crowd who is coming next. More on the ball than any comparable

SWEDISH FANS GREET THEIR HEROES: NOTE WHOSE NAME COMES FIRST!

audience in the world, the enthusiastic, well-informed Swedes, 'We Love Milton' banners at the ready, lustily hail their heroes long before they have even jumped a fence.

It is an experience which would reduce a nervous horse to a jibbing wreck. Not so Milton. The adulation merely makes him jump better. 'It sharpens him up,' says John, adding with his customary understatement, 'It's quite nice that the crowd's behind you. I wouldn't say that it gives you confidence exactly, but the one thing about the crowd there is that you can make a mistake and they don't boo you out of the ring.'

As holders of the World Cup John and Milton were automatically qualified for the 1991 final in Gothenburg. But John, as was his custom, took Milton to the last few European qualifiers as part of his early season campaign.

For his initial outing of the year, Milton was the star attraction at a special charity event staged at the South View Equestrian Centre in Wettenhall, Cheshire, to raise money for Liverpool's Alder Hey Children's Hospital. There he gave everyone value for money by taking the feature event, worth £2,000 to the winner. A few days later he was in s'Hertogenbosch where he finished among the minor prize-money earners in the puissance. This event, with its big wall, is very much the preserve of a few specialist jumpers and is not contested seriously by riders on their Grand Prix horses. But sometimes it makes a useful warm-up class and a horse such as Milton is usually pulled out after the first or, at most, the second round.

Despite his longer-than-usual winter break, Milton proved himself to be fit and in splendid form by finishing runner-up in the World Cup qualifier, beaten in the jump-off by Walzerkönig by a mere 0.14 seconds. The following week, returning to Dortmund, the scene of his triumph 12 months earlier, he won one class and was fourth in the World Cup. Again he jumped a double clear round and was beaten only by the clock. This time victory went to Norton de Rhuys, with Brazil's Nelson Pessoa placed second on Special Envoy, the former Swiss international rider Heidi Robbiani's grand horse, and Mon Santa third.

Milton's last appearance before the final was in the Paris qualifier, which he was attempting to win for the third time in four years. On this occasion, though, it was Hubert Bourdy's turn to play the ace. In the jump-off he threw down the challenge of a clear round in a very fast time, thanks in large measure to a brilliantly executed turn to the last fence. Going in hot pursuit, John was looking to make a similarly quick turn but Milton arrived at the penultimate obstacle not quite straight, got too close and, although he bettered Morgat's time, four faults dropped him to fourth place.

There could be no doubt that the grey was in fine fettle for his forthcoming attempt to become only the second horse to defend successfully his Volvo title. Sadly, Big Ben was again unfit to contest the final. But there was no shortage of opposition from the rest of the world. The Europeans, though, were quietly confident of once more staving off the North American challenge.

And so to Gothenburg, very much the spiritual home of the World Cup. It was Volvo chief Pehr G Gyllenhammar, drawn into the horse world during the 1970s by his teenage daughters, who was largely instrumental in creating this hugely successful international show in a hitherto totally unhorsey city. In less than two decades it has become a mecca for the world's top riders, with a crowd that is undoubtedly the most enthusiastic and most welcoming of any in the world.

Milton had a satisfactory, if less than sparkling, first-day warm up. John described his performance as 'a bit casual' after he took a pole off the sixth fence, but was confident that he would evince more interest over the bigger fences in the speed leg.

However, John's defence of his title did not exactly get off to a flying start. His name emerged fourth in the draw from the 42 starters, even less propitious than the previous year. Philosophical as ever, John merely shrugged and said, 'I shall just have to go in and do my own thing.'

Despite his early draw he managed to see a couple of rounds on the TV monitor in the collecting ring before his turn came. Neither was very inspiring. But as the competition progressed, the course – provided by local man Roland Nilsson – came in for a good deal of praise. Paul Schockemöhle, with two top horses involved, said it tested all aspects of a horse's jumping ability: there were a good many turns, a long gallop, a double of planks and a narrow vertical after a big double of oxers to finish. Its complexities were such that only four horses jumped clear rounds.

Milton set the ball rolling in fine style. John decided to take special care over the first half-dozen fences which he described as 'tricky'. He executed a brilliant turn to number six, a triple bar after the double of planks and thereafter was able to put his foot down rather more. After another tight turn from the eighth, he saw a long stride to the ninth, a second triple bar set at the far end of the arena and Milton took a flier at it, saving valuable time. Steadying for the big double of oxers and the following vertical, John was home clear in 60.48 seconds. It put him in the lead until Franke Sloothaak and Walzerkönig came in and knocked the time down to 59.31. Finally, Schockemöhle's second stable jockey Otto Becker on Pamina, a pair who had gone well in Stockholm the year before, reduced the time further to 58.13 and that proved to be the winning performance. Nick Skelton on Grand Slam, quickly recovered from a crashing fall the previous day, produced the only other clear; they finished fourth in a time marginally slower than Milton's.

Third place, thanks to a well-judged piece of tactical riding and despite the bad draw, left John feeling reasonably satisfied as he turned his attention to the second leg. As usual the fences would be bigger all round and the British pair would be in their element. Jumping in reverse order to the first day, John would have ample time to watch his rivals cope with the course's complexities.

Roland Nilsson admitted afterwards to being alarmed when the first two horses went clear. He was hoping for eight or nine clears in round one followed by half-a-dozen in the first jump-off but it began to look as if he made things too easy. He need not have worried. It soon became obvious that he had judged it correctly. Faults were spread evenly around the course, there was no bogey fence and he achieved his hoped-for eight clears in round one, with six getting through to the final jump-off.

Milton, reported by John to be jumping really well, had a most unlucky four faults at the 1.60-metre wall, the penultimate fence, and could finish only equal ninth. He gave the coping the merest nudge with a front foot, not sufficient to dislodge it but enough to move it slightly forward. But as he began his descent he caught it with his hindlegs and down it came. With it, John felt, had gone his chance of retaining the Cup.

From the stands, it had looked highly likely that the barrage of flashbulbs, set off

JOHN AND MILTON OVERCAME A POTENTIALLY DISASTROUS EARLY DRAW TO WIN THE 1991 WORLD CUP. AFTERWARDS FORMER OLYMPIC CHAMPION WILLIAM STEINKRAUS DESCRIBED THEM AS 'TRULY THE TOUGHEST COMBINATION IN THE WORLD'

by Milton's adoring but misguided fans every time he jumped, might have distracted him. John felt he had just been unlucky, though he admits that flashbulbs can be a nuisance, particularly at the end of the arena when horse and rider are jumping towards them:

> On the odd occasion I have felt that Milton's been distracted but not really that often and not enough to cause him to make a bad mistake. But it can be momentarily blinding. When you're in there you need 100 per cent concentration and it doesn't take much to distract a horse.

All was not lost, and by the end of the competition, won in superb style by the veteran 55-year-old Brazilian Nelson Pessoa on Special Envoy, who had finished only 16th in the speed leg, John found himself still in third place. Coincidentally, none of the leading combinations from day one had produced a clear. Otto Becker, with four faults in the first round, was still leading and so had the zero score for the start of day three.

VICTORY IN THE 1991
WORLD CUP FINAL IN
GOTHENBURG EARNED
MILTON £58,589,
INCLUDING A CAR, HIS
NINTH IN WORLD CUP
COMPETITIONS

The Brazilian was lying second on 1.00, while John and Frenchman Roger-Yves Bost on Norton de Rhuys, third in the second leg, each had 1.50.

In retrospect, Milton's brick out of the wall did him no harm at all for it saved him one, possibly two, further rounds and ensured that he was fresh for leg three. The first-round course, deliberately made less gruelling than in Dortmund 12 months before, was described by John as 'difficult enough but not a killer.' He and Milton coped impressively with its technical problems, moving up into second place thanks to a faultless performance. Special Envoy, also clear, took over the leading position vacated by Pamina, who was caught out by the planks in the middle of the treble and slipped to third.

With just 1.00 fault separating the two leading horses, the tension became almost unbearable as John approached the first fence on his final round. No one would be less than delighted if victory went to the stylish Brazilian, no crowd more generous with its reception than this one. But it was impossible to escape the feeling that deep down virtually everyone was willing the great Milton to complete a historic double here on the World Cup's home soil.

Nilsson's last course was short – only nine obstacles – but again technically testing. Milton took it all in his stride, sweeping through the finish clear to an unbelievable ovation. Bunches of tulips came raining down from the stands – an unprecedented occurrence in a show jumping arena – as the grey, looking pleased if startled, made his exit. A buzz went round the stadium as the crowd began to sense that victory for the favourite was now a distinct possibility. But if anyone could cope with the pressure of going last it was the remarkable Brazilian. Still riding with the flair of a man half his age, 'Neco' had competed in his first Olympics before John had even learnt to walk, let alone sit on a horse. He knew exactly what it was like to be in his rival's shoes, too, for he had gone into the last round of the 1984 final just 1.00 fault behind the eventual winner, the young Canadian, Mario Deslauriers and Aramis. This time it was he who had the whip hand. Another clear round would take the World Cup to South America for the first time.

A tense silence descended on the Scandinavium as he approached the first fence. It did not not last long. The writing was on the wall as he turned into the double at three, an oxer to a vertical on a long stride. Special Envoy was a fraction wrong at the first, cleverly got himself out of trouble but paid the penalty at the second. In a few swift seconds possible victory turned to defeat, by 5.00 faults to 1.50.

It would be an understatement to say that the crowd erupted. There were sympathetic cheers for the defeated Brazilian, ecstatic ones for the victorious Milton, the only horse that day to complete a double clear. When the British pair came in for their solo bow John, normally so undemonstrative, waved his hat to the delighted crowd and twice asked Milton to perform his party piece: a leap off the ground and a kick-back which closely resembles the capriole performed by one or two other famous grey horses, those at Vienna's Spanish Riding School. It is something which John found quite by accident that Milton can do on request and it never fails to capture the hearts of the crowd.

Youngsters at the ringside competed energetically for flowers thrown to them by John from his victory bouquet. British team manager Ronnie Massarella was visibly moved by what old hands agreed was the most emotional jumping victory in a very long time. For Ronnie, only recently back in action after a winter of illness, it was the best tonic in the world.

William Steinkraus, former United States Olympic champion, summed up the universal admiration of the experts in his customary eloquent style: 'To come from behind like that is a tremendous test of technical resourcefulness and character and John did it perfectly. The courses set many problems. John made all the right decisions and executed them faultlessly. He and Milton are truly the toughest combination in the world.'

CHAPTER 16

HORSES ARE NOT MACHINES

After a break of several weeks following his exertions in Gothenburg, Milton made a spectacular comeback to competition. John took in the Royal Bath and West Show as a warm up en route to Hickstead where his premier objective was the Grand Prix, worth £21,000 to the winner. Third in 1989 and runner-up in 1990, John felt that it was time he and Milton scooped the big prize.

Despite the presence of so many of his regular rivals – Jos Lansink, Nelson Pessoa, David Broome, his own brother Michael – and many more of the best known riders in Europe, he ultimately found himself engaged in a battle royal with the remarkable Mark Todd. The British-based New Zealander, twice Olympic three-day event champion, was widely regarded as the greatest all-round horseman in the world. He had entered his Barcelona show jumping prospect Double Take, a horse bred in his home country as a shepherd's hack but now an accomplished international performer. He readily admitted that Double Take is no Milton, but Mark's genius is such that he conjured a tremendously fast clear round out of him in the jump-off to take the lead with only four horses left to go.

John, starting immediately afterwards, knew he had to pull something special out of the bag to better the New Zealander's time. As he explained afterwards, the course did not really suit Milton because there was too much galloping involved. By the halfway stage he was already slightly down on the clock, so he decided to chance jumping the second last, a big oxer, at an angle. It is at moments like this that Milton's tremendous scope comes into full play. He stretched out over it in breathtaking style, neatly executed a sharp turn to the final fence, landed clear and stopped the clock in a time that was nearly three-quarters of a second faster than Double Take's. None of those who came after – Eddie Macken, Michael Whitaker and Nelson Pessoa – were either clear or close to his time.

In response to suggestions that he should perhaps emulate Mark Todd and take up a second sport, John shook his head emphatically: 'I'm not taking up three-day eventing – it looks too dangerous to me!'

Two days later Milton again outshone his rival, jumping an immaculate double clear round in the Nations Cup for the fourth year running. However, in the absence of quite such faultless support from his team-mates, it was not enough to keep the Edward, Prince of Wales Cup at home. France, having finished on level terms with the host nation after the two rounds, forged ahead with three successive clears in the jump-off. Milton was not required to jump again.

He missed the Royal International that summer, going instead to the Nations Cup meetings in St Gallen and Aachen, part of the build-up programme mapped out for the European Championships. At the Swiss show, where Britain finished second, he completed the team event with just four faults. In Aachen, where torrential rain had made the going atrocious, he made light of the conditions, jumping another superb double clear, the tenth of his career, though the team could finish only third.

On the first day at the German show Milton found himself out in the arena receiving a prize he had not won, which must have given him pause for thought. Was he to be rewarded now merely for being there? John had ridden Gammon to victory in the first big competition of the show, but because the brown gelding tends to have a rush of blood to the head at awards ceremonies his rider decided not to risk taking him in. It would, he said, do Milton good anyway to take a look at the arena before he had to jump. He had not been to Aachen since 1987, and there is never any harm in letting a horse take a look at his surroundings, with all their attendant distractions, before asking them to go in and concentrate on big fences.

As his final outing before going to La Baule, in France, to defend his European title, Milton went to the Great Yorkshire Show where he thrilled his local fans, not to mention his Yorkshire rider, by winning the feature event, the Cock o' the North Championship.

It augured well for the European Championships; yet they turned out to be something of a disappointment. Two fine World Cup wins, numerous clear rounds in World Cup qualifiers, Grands Prix and Nations Cups – had we all come to expect too much, to fall into the trap of looking upon Milton as the ultimate jumping machine? To finish first, equal seventh and equal sixth in three legs of a Championship should surely not be considered disappointing. Yet, where Milton is concerned, to come away without an individual medal was certainly just that.

On day one there was no hint of the drama to come. Blessed with a late draw, John and Milton blazed round the 14-fence course. He just rattled the last, but was home clear in the fastest time, more than three seconds ahead of his nearest rival. Even John was surprised by his time: 'I tried to treat it as a normal competition. I didn't realise I was as fast as I was.' He undoubtedly saved time by taking a stride out going to fence 11, a gambit which he rightly considered safer than opting for a tight turn to the next fence.

Day two of the Nations Cup was less happy. During the break between the two rounds it was announced that the leading French course designer, Philippe Gayot, who had been replaced at the last moment by Switzerland's Paul Weier, had finally lost his courageous fight against cancer. The loss of such a popular figure in the sport did nothing to enhance the spirits of Milton's supporters, who were already beginning to realise that their hero was losing his grip on the title.

It was two years (the last European Championships, in fact) since he had failed to jump at least one clear round in a team contest. Now, when he needed a two-round total of four or better to retain his lead, he lowered a rail each time and was overtaken by Dutchman Piet Raymakers on the brilliant young mare, Ratina Z. Both of Milton's mistakes came at combinations: in the first round, part A of a double set of verticals at the sixth, in the second, the oxer going into the treble. If only Milton had scored one of his devastating double clears, Britain would have won a record fourth consecutive team title. Now they were lucky to hang on to the silver, finishing as they did behind the much improved, well-mounted Dutch squad, and less than a fence ahead of the Swiss.

Individually, of course, John and Milton had been in a similar position two years previously and had still succeeded in powering their way to the gold medal on the final day. But hopes that they would repeat this feat in La Baule were swiftly dispelled in the first round of the third leg. Milton, it will be remembered, had astounded everyone by faulting at the water in Rotterdam. Now he did it again. And, to make matters worse, he lowered a rail as well. Just as in the Nations Cup, the fault came at what had always appeared to be one of Milton's least problematical fences, an oxer. Suddenly he was looking fallible. Eight faults (no one, not even John, could remember the last time the horse had made two mistakes in the same round) dropped him to third place behind Ratina Z, and, edging relentlessly up the scoreboard, the World Champions Eric Navet and Quito de Baussy.

The title holders were evidently beginning to struggle. Another fence down in the second round, this time the oxer going out of the treble, and it was all over. A three-day total of 20 faults dropped Milton to fifth. Quito de Baussy, whose faultless efforts in legs two and three more than made up for a bad performance in the speed leg, made the Frenchman the first rider since Gerd Wiltfang in 1978/79 to win World and European titles in successive years. Walzerkönig pulled right up to take the silver and Jos Lansink with Egano overtook his compatriot Piet Raymakers and Ratina Z to win the bronze. Quito de Baussy was the clear winner on 12.22, his score from the speed leg. But the scores for the minor medals were close. Less than four faults – one fence – separated Walzerkönig, on 16.59, from Milton. Somehow, though, that did not seem to matter. Milton's mistakes had taken everyone by surprise and everyone wanted to be in at the inquest.

John was at a loss for an explanation. 'He wasn't jumping badly but he was just lacking that little bit extra somewhere. He didn't feel tired,' he added, pointing out that he had only done four shows since Gothenburg. Rider error probably accounted for his mistake at the water, which was on a related distance to a double of verticals, but John was surprised that Milton had taken the front rail off the oxer in the second round: 'Coming out of a combination is usually the least of my problems.' True, the weather had been blisteringly hot. And Milton had been lying down in his box more than usual, not a good sign. Was he adversely affected by the weather? Was he simply unwell? Blood tests taken when he returned home revealed nothing out of the ordinary.

Doreen Bradley felt that he had, perhaps, done too much in his warm-up show,

WHERE DID YOU GET
THOSE HATS? AFTER
WINNING THE GRAND PRIX
AT THE HICKSTEAD
NATIONS CUP MEETING IN
1991, MILTON GREETS
THREE ELEGANT
REPRESENTATIVES OF THE
SPONSORS, EMIRATE
AIRLINES

the Great Yorkshire; and that he had gone too fast in the speed leg of the Championship, which could have taken the edge off him. No one will ever know for sure. We had all expected him to be his usual brilliant self. By his exceptional standards these were a couple of off days.

After a holiday he jumped in Mondorf before setting off on his annual visit to Calgary. If anyone had begun to feel that he was a spent force, his performances there proved otherwise. A clear first round in the Nations Cup set Britain on the path to a third consecutive victory and he was not required to start second time. In the Grand Prix, won by his old rivals, Ian Millar and Big Ben, with the only double clear round, he recorded the second-fastest two-round total of four faults to pick up third prize, worth a cool £37,202. A week later at the San Marino Nations Cup meeting he added another £21,920 to his tally by finishing runner-up in the Grand Prix there. As a bare statistic it looked like just another nicely judged effort by John and his wonder horse. The truth behind it was much more dramatic.

The San Marino Show was a glamorous addition to the international calendar. For Italian tenor Luciano Pavarotti it was the fulfilment of a long-held dream. A tremendous horse enthusiast, with his own string of show jumpers, he had an ambition to host an international show at his equestrian centre in his home town of Modena. Since Italy already has a Nations Cup Show in Rome, there was no question of the FEI allocating another to the same country, but there were no objections when the application was made in San Marino's name. And hey presto, 'the Pavarotti Show' as it was immediately dubbed, came into being.

Milton was one of the European horses destined to go straight to Modena from Calgary. It was a long, arduous journey, made doubly wearing by an unconscionable delay in Milan while the relevant paperwork was processed. The horses were unloaded from the plane and put in their lorries, where they then stayed, in the heat, for the best part of eight hours. Not surprisingly they were tired and dehydrated by the time they were installed in their stables at Modena. Milton picked up quickly enough, and because he had arrived a couple of days before the show was due to start, he had a reasonable time in which to recuperate. John restricted him to walking-out exercise for the first two days, he received regular vet checks and although he was not asked to start in the Nations Cup, he jumped in a small class and did fine.

He duly took his place in the line-up for the Grand Prix. Unfortunately the weather had obviously mistaken the show for an outdoor operatic performance in England, and behaved accordingly. Although by the time of the Grand Prix, the ground was beginning to dry out, it was still sticky and with so many horses competing, the surface at the take-offs had inevitably become deep. It is in such conditions that things can go wrong for horses, and it was Milton's turn to draw the short straw.

He was one of only two to conquer the conditions and the courses, to jump a brace of clear rounds and go through to a jump-off against the clock. Egano, ridden by Jos Lansink, was the other. Egano, always a dangerous opponent, went first and was clear again in a fast time. John set off in pursuit. But he had barely got going before he felt Milton's legs get stuck in the mud on the take-off side of the second fence which he could not avoid hitting. 'I didn't realise that he'd overreached, but there was no point in carrying on so I retired. It was as I was walking out of the ring that I realised there was blood flowing from his leg.'

It was a classic 'muddy ground' injury: the horse has difficulty getting his forefeet out of the ground, his hindfeet come down before he has chance to get his forefeet out of the way, and an iron-clad hind hoof strikes into a front heel. In Milton's case it was the heel of the leg which he had injured all those years before while being clipped. He had struck into an artery, there was a lot of blood and the wound had to be stitched. Doreen Bradley wanted him to remain in Modena to recuperate but, although he is not the bravest of horses at such times, John felt he was fit enough to be boxed up and taken home with the others.

Once the wound had healed he was soon sound again and was put back into light work. But only a couple of days later, shortly before the Horse of the Year Show, John sensed that he did not feel quite right.

It's possible he bruised his pastern when he overreached, or it could have been something quite different – he could even have done it at home in his box. It was strange that he was sound for a week or so and then wasn't.

There was a slight swelling in his pastern but a precautionary X-ray revealed nothing. There was no choice but to give him a long lay-off while it righted itself. As John says, 'With a cut, it heals up and that's that. But when it's something you can't see it's better to give a horse longer rather than start working him too soon.'

There was an amusing footnote to the Modena show. John was presented with a £35,000 Maserati. He was not quite sure why, but it seems to have been a cumulative award based on performances in several top Grands Prix, including Aachen and Calgary. Impressed though he was with the car, he did not think his wife, Clare, would find it suitable for ferrying small children to school. 'I did ask them whether they made a turbo, four-wheel drive estate version,' he said, 'but I don't think they do.'

Milton's enforced absence from Wembley meant that his stranglehold on the Masters was broken. He did not jump again until Frankfurt in early December. There John gave him a couple of cautious preliminary outings and he finished in the money on both occasions. He felt fit and well and it was decided to take him to the big show in Paris a week later. A further warm-up outing showed him to be in fine form and he joined the line-up for the Renault Grand Prix.

A clear round took him through to the jump-off; a further clear earned him top prize of nearly £13,000. The points he earned, added to those amassed by John's other entry Grannusch, ensured that the Yorkshireman went home with yet another car. Among those floundering behind him were the World and European Champions, Eric Navet with Quito de Baussy.

Milton was back in the winner's enclosure, where he belonged, though not before giving his connections another fright by injuring himself in his stable during the night before the Grand Prix. For a horse who is always keen to get his nose into people's pockets in search of Polo Mints, he showed little inclination to do so on the Sunday morning and on close inspection was discovered to have had his tongue bitten.

MILTON LOOKING READY FOR A SIESTA AT LA BAULE

'He must have had a piece taken out by his neighbour when they had their heads over their doors during the night,' Doreen Bradley said. 'He was probably trying to steal someone else's food.'

Although it was obviously sore, the injured tongue did not seem to be causing him any problems with his bit and, having captured the big prize in Paris, he travelled home to Olympia. It was his first appearance at a British indoor show since Wembley 1990 and he was accorded a right royal welcome to which he responded by winning the big jump-off class on the opening night.

Despite his restricted season, yet again he wound up the year as Britain's leading money winner, with £193,985 in the bank.

CHAPTER 17

OWNING MILTON

If anyone had told young Tom Bradley, when he decided all those years ago to 'tag along' with Doreen and her horses, that he would spend his retirement travelling the world to watch show jumping he would have thought them daft in the head. Yet here he is today, jetting around the international circuit with his wife – 'not so much a couple of wrinklies as a couple of crumblies,' as she puts it. Ask Tom where he is off to next and he invariably nods in the direction of Doreen and says, 'You'd better ask the boss. I just make sure my suitcase is packed.' But clearly he enjoys the involvement in it all and there is still a sense of wonder that he and his wife own a horse who gives delight to tens of thousands of people all over the world – and at the same time keeps the family supplied with, amongst other things, a succession of splendid new cars.

Undoubtedly Milton has made the Bradleys' years as senior citizens more exciting than they could ever have imagined possible. Though if his fans find watching Milton in action an emotionally draining experience, imagine how much worse it must be for his owners. Tom recalls how Doreen used to pretend to be watching him very closely but in fact was really going by the applause. 'I've seen her to all intents and purposes concentrating hard, but the jumping's down below us and she's looking up somewhere else! I've caught hold of her hand when the tension's starting to build and it's been absolutely soaked.'

Doreen claims that she does not get as nervous now as she used to, though she does still find that a rise in tension seems, strangely enough, to produce a rise in temperature in the arena. People sitting with them in the stands start laughing when they hear her say, 'Gosh, isn't it getting warm in here.'

Among the numerous exciting moments which Milton has given them, several stand out for the Bradleys as being especially memorable. 'I've always said that the greatest moment for me was when he won the Grand Prix in Gothenburg in 1987,' says Doreen. It was Caroline's birthday so that was a really special moment. 'And of course we were delighted when he won the King George in 1990 because it meant that Caroline had then, as it were, won both the Queen's Cup and the King George.'

The King George V Gold Cup is one of, if not the, most valuable, handsome and coveted trophies in the world of sport. Depicting St George slaying the dragon, it is a sculpture cast in 18ct gold and was first presented at the International Horse Show, Olympia, in 1911 to mark the beginning of the reign of the new monarch. Except in 1947 and 1948, it has always been restricted to men riders, the ladies' equivalent being the Queen Elizabeth II Cup which was first competed for in 1949 as the Princess Elizabeth Cup. Caroline had won the Queen's Cup twice, once with

Marius and once with Tigre, hence the Bradleys' particular pleasure at seeing Milton win the King's. The trophy is of course for perpetual competition and Doreen regrets that no memento is presented to the winning connections – 'just a spoon to put on the table would be nice.' It is also priceless and not the sort of thing to have standing around in your sitting-room. The Bradleys once returned home to find that their house had been broken into and many of Caroline's trophies stolen. Not surprisingly they would never risk having something like the King's Cup on display. Most winning owners leave it safely locked up in the vaults of the Crown Jewellers. A few years ago one rider who did decide to have the trophy at home said his wife was so scared that they might be burgled, every time he stayed away at a show overnight she took it to bed with her.

Milton's double gold in the European Championships, held in the same arena (Rotterdam) where Caroline had won a European team gold medal, was another special moment for the Bradleys, as was the Grand Prix at Hickstead in 1991: 'You feel particularly pleased when he does something in his own country. You want the horse to win for his own sake, and you want him to win for the rider's sake – and of course when he does hit a fence you also feel that he's let the crowd down.'

Basically it is John Whitaker who decides on a day-to-day basis where Milton is going to jump but that does not prevent people from making special requests to the Bradleys to allow him to go to such and such a show. Milton's participation, like Desert Orchid's on a racecourse in recent years, can materially affect the 'gate'. When the phone rings at the Bradley home it is quite likely to be a show organiser pleading, 'Couldn't we have him just for the little classes?' (if all these requests were acceded to, Milton would be worn out in no time at all) or else someone trying to buy him. 'We have been bombarded with offers, astronomical offers, Doreen admits, 'from all over, including the Americans – and they are still bombarding.' The answer is always the same: 'Milton is not for sale.'

Doreen feels that despite his outstanding achievements the horse has not been appreciated in Britain as much as he deserves and equestrian journalists who have followed his international career at first hand would be inclined to agree. Athletes in other sports and, to draw a closer analogy, racehorses often feature on the front pages of national newspapers. But when did Milton, the only horse in Europe to win two World Cups, ever have his photo on a front page, except in the equestrian press? The Bradleys were castigated for not letting him go to the Seoul Olympics, they were accused of letting down the country but, asks Doreen, does the country really care all that much? It has to be said that Milton is much more of a celebrity abroad than he is on home territory, partly because the major events, with their generous prize money, attract much bigger crowds (does the fact that they are, generally speaking, staged in better facilities have something to do with this?) and partly because they are reported much more lavishly.

When Milton won his second World Cup Final, in Gothenburg in 1991, a crowd of 11,000 gave him a standing ovation and the following morning his picture was emblazoned across the front pages of virtually every Swedish newspaper. Although the British daily papers all had correspondents on the spot, Milton's many home fans had to rummage through the regular sports pages to find the modest amounts of text allocated to this tremendous victory. The previous year, within a few weeks of the conclusion of the World Equestrian Games in Stockholm a Swedish publisher brought out a commemorative, lavishly illustrated book devoted not, as one might have expected, to the gold medallist, Eric Navet's Quito de Baussy, but to the runner-up, Milton. It sold out in six weeks. He is quite simply by far and away the most photogenic and best-loved horse performing in any sport anywhere yet sports editors in his own country have largely failed to exploit him.

Which brings us to the general question of exploitation and the 'Milton industry'. Without doubt a great many people have cashed in on Milton's eye-catching appearance and tremendous public appeal. Wherever they go the Bradleys see pictures of him advertising shows, or reproduced on the covers of programmes and on souvenir posters. As a general rule they do not mind because they accept that it helps promote the shows in question but people undoubtedly take advantage and occasionally it can be more than a little irritating. As when, at a show such as Vienna, the official hotel 'has pictures of Milton plastered all over the place. We're still paying our £100 a night for a room, but they're using our horse to advertise. That to me is very annoying,' says Doreen. On another occasion a show did take the trouble to phone the Bradleys to ask if they minded Milton appearing on the front of their programme – about which they were perfectly happy – but then used a particularly unflattering picture which Doreen felt did not do the horse justice. Sometimes, too, she feels that owners should be included more in social events when their horses are jumping for the British team.

Travelling the world with Milton may seem glamorous but, as the Bradleys point out, it cost in the region of £2,000 just to go to Stockholm for the 1990 Games and for two 'crumblies' the problems of travelling around do not get any easier. On the other hand, there are occasional nice surprises. Doreen recalls a couple of shows which do not exactly send out free invitations to owners but who do 'surprise you when you go to pay the bill by waiving it. We fell over with excitement!'

Owning Milton undoubtedly brings the Bradleys an enormous amount of pleasure. It also brings with it an enormous sense of responsibility and constant, might one say 'nagging', worries about his welfare. Is he being asked to do too much; is he safe being transported around the world by road, sea and air; is the ground suitable for him to jump on; is the show stabling comfortable?

Milton's career since he joined John Whitaker has been remarkably trouble free but the one occasion on which he did contract a virus, in the winter of 1990, was,

Doreen feels, the direct result of the considerable pressures of campaigning on the indoor winter circuit: not too much jumping, but simply too much travelling and too much changing from one environment to another. At the beginning of that winter Milton competed in Stuttgart before going out to Vienna and then back to Maastricht. 'It's a long way to Vienna,' said Doreen. 'One forgets just how far east it is. The weather was very cold there and the stabling is in a stuffy underground car park, which is most unsuitable. Milton caught a "bug" there and then wasn't well when he went back to Holland where it was much warmer. All this must have an effect on horses, just as it does on humans.' Milton's illness was diagnosed as a respiratory virus and he was given a good holiday, 'which never does any harm'.

There was an amusing (though not to Milton) tailpiece, or perhaps one should say headpiece, to this episode: he became bald. All the hair round his ears fell out. Fortunately it was only a temporary thing and as he recovered from the virus so his hair grew again.

For his public one of Milton's greatest charms is his rocking-horse canter, which seems to be accentuated by his flowing white mane. However, it is not for aesthetic reasons that his mane is, unlike most other show jumpers, left unplaited, though Doreen admits that 'he would look silly now if they started plaiting him – he wouldn't have half the character.' A plaited mane has become very much a part of the accepted turnout at big events but Doreen firmly believes that horses are better left unplaited, except perhaps if their mane is very unruly or they have a particularly ugly neck. She agrees with Caroline's theory that plaiting a top horse just before he is about to compete is unfair. 'You've got the girl groom worrying the horse before he starts, standing over him and fussing him at the very time when you should be letting him relax. You're bothering him at the worst possible moment. Plaits must also be uncomfortable for the horse, especially when he stretches out his neck over a fence.' Milton proved this point in no uncertain terms. He always used to be plaited when he first went to John's yard, but not only did he not much care for the actual plaiting process but after a while he began to shake his head constantly when he was jumping. Eventually John decided to leave his mane loose.

A horse's well-being, particularly when he is travelling, is very much in the hands of his groom and, as Tom says, if you haven't got a groom who takes real care 'you might as well pack it in. Milton is lucky to have been looked after by two such good girls as Penny and Mandy.'

Doreen is a great believer in the prevention of problems and 'goes mad' if she sees horses being ridden out on the road without kneeboots or being schooled without protective boots. Jumping on bad ground is another very real worry but unfortunately something which cannot always be avoided outdoors if weather conditions change during a show. Milton's one injury sustained while jumping was, significantly, the result of an overreach at Modena in 1991 caused by his inability to get his feet out of the heavy going. When you get to indoor shows you do at least know what you're going to jump on, she says. 'You're not usually subject to funny conditions and the horses get a rhythm going. They mightn't come out and win at, say, Hickstead next time but it's better than getting stuck in the mud as Milton did in Modena.'

By far the biggest trauma associated with owning Milton came in 1988 when the Bradleys' refusal to make him available for the Olympic Games in Seoul became headline news. The dispute ran for many months, with the Bradleys cast very much as the villains of the piece. It is a subject which has been endlessly discussed, analysed and expounded upon, but no book about the horse would be complete without a further resumé of the pertinent facts.

When John Whitaker was given the ride on Milton in 1985 it was with the stipulation that there were three events in which the Bradleys did not wish the horse to participate: The Suffolk County Show, for obvious reasons; The Hickstead Derby, whose massive bank with its steep 10ft 6in descent they considered too dangerous; and the Olympic Games. John accepted these conditions as part of the deal and has always respected them meticulously.

However, to the selectors, Milton's absence from the Olympic team was unthinkable. And they were convinced that the Bradleys could and should be influenced to change their minds. At a time when Britain was not exactly bristling with horses of Olympic standard, the grey represented the team's best medal-winning chance, particularly in the individual event. Pressure was put upon Doreen and Tom to think again. The whole matter became more and more acrimonious, and increasingly stressful to the Bradleys. It finally came to a head at the Hickstead Nations Cup meeting during the first week in June and at the Royal International, which took place at the National Exhibition Centre, Birmingham, ten days later.

At Hickstead the selectors revealed that since Milton was not being made available for the Olympics, he would be banned from forthcoming Nations Cup teams, which would be restricted to those horses short-listed for the Games. It was a decision which very nearly lost Milton from the British team for all time. The horse had originally gone to John's stables on the understanding that he would never be taken from him and given to another British rider. That, however, did not preclude his owners from offering him to someone overseas and, although it was not public knowledge at the time, the decision to bar the horse from the Nations Cup teams so rankled with the Bradleys that this nearly came about.

Then at Birmingham John's fellow competitors joined the campaign. In an open letter to the Bradleys, the eight other short-listed riders urged them to change their minds, indicating that any one of them would gladly relinquish their chance of a place in the team in favour of John and Milton.

Speaking to the equestrian press, who wrote about little else for several days,

Nick Skelton said he believed that Milton's absence meant that the team had gone from 'a gold-medal position to fighting for a bronze.' David Broome was of the opinion that 'Milton is fifty per cent of any team and his absence is a disaster.' He confirmed that 'each one of us would be prepared to stand down to have Milton on the team.' He added that the British Equestrian Federation had laid out a lot of money in sending Milton abroad with the team in the past and this had not exactly been detrimental to the horse's owners. The implication was that in return they should say thank you for this backing by permitting the horse to go to Seoul. But the Bradleys stood firm, reminding everyone of their original well-publicised decision: 'He was never available for selection to go to Korea,' and adding 'if the Games had been closer to home it would be a different matter.'

The reasons behind this decision, which were given regular airings at the time, concerned Milton's safety and future and centered on the fact that as he was the Bradley's last link with Caroline's horses they did not wish to involve him in unnecessary risk. The journey to Korea was far longer than most other trips he had made to overseas events; despite the stringent quarantine conditions specially devised for incoming horses, there was always the possibility that he might pick up a virus in the Far East, and the Olympics had long since earned a reputation for shortening a horse's jumping career. In fact, by that time the 'killer courses' favoured in previous Games were largely a thing of the past, but it was still considered too much of a risk.

Certainly there was an element of truth in these strictures levelled at the Olympics. But for the Bradleys there were other, more personal, reasons, behind their decision which were only hinted at. Caroline had said, 'No horse of mine will ever go to the Olympics.' For her parents the memory was still fresh of the heartache she had suffered in 1972 concerning Wood Nymph, of her enforced adoption of professional status, and of the heartbreak over Tigre who was originally put up for sale because, Doreen recalls, Mr Bannocks 'wanted the horse to be ridden in the Olympics'.

Right up to the last minute the selectors refused to believe that the Bradleys could not be prevailed upon to change their minds. Milton was even included in the *Olympic Handbook* published by the BEF, and featuring all the short-listed horses and riders, to help raise money for the Olympic Fund.

Throughout the feud John Whitaker maintaining a dignified near silence. Of course he was disappointed, just as he had been when Britain had boycotted the Moscow Olympics and he lost the chance of a medal with his previous top horse, Ryan's Son. During the Royal International he said, when pressed, 'From my point of view the disappointing thing is that I would have such a good chance **now**. In four years time Milton might not be as good.' Which is exactly what happened with Ryan's Son. But John respected the Bradleys' wishes and felt that heaping pressure upon them was not the way to go about things.

Apart from John, the one constant unmoved factor in the entire unfortunate business was Milton himself. Blissfully unaware that he was at the centre of so much ill-feeling and controversy, he jumped the only double clear round in the Hickstead Nations Cup, which must have aggrieved the selectors no end. At Birmingham he won the *Daily Mail* Cup on the opening day, finished runner-up in the King's Cup

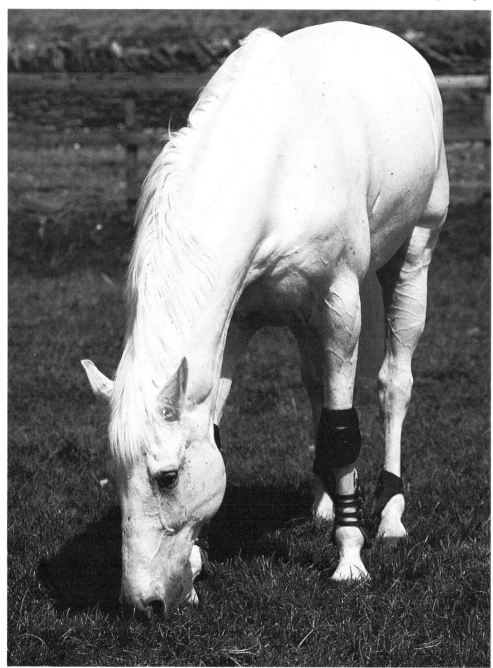

RELAXING AT HOME IN YORKSHIRE. EATING IS MILTON'S NUMBER ONE FAVOURITE PASTIME

and took the Everest Grand Prix at the final performance. John, the total professional, proved that he could banish the whole unpleasant business from his mind when it mattered most: 'It really doesn't make any difference when I am competing'.

Indeed, one thing that has always given Doreen Bradley particular pleasure is to watch the sheer skill and professionalism of the handful of top British riders and to see their tremendous team spirit at the big international championships. 'Michael [John's brother] is a beautiful rider. I love the sight of him on a horse – except of course when he's trying to win a class that Milton's in! Good luck to the boys: they're young, they're brilliant and they're going to be brilliant for another 20 years so they shouldn't ever have to mess about with bad horses.' It annoys her to hear people from their own country asking why it is always be the same riders who compete abroad:

> They are only there because they are so brilliant. And take Nick Skelton. Okay, Nick will come in and try and beat John and Michael – they all try to win – but if he's out of the jump-off he'll be the first to run over and give John advice. That's far more valuable than the gratuitous type of advice you sometimes get from people who just come out to the odd big championship show and then start saying, "Oh, give him another jump", that sort of thing.
>
> Riders all talk the same language even if they don't all work their horses the same way. I find it fascinating to watch them, not only our boys but people like Franke Sloothaak and the Dutch riders. It's significant that the Germans always say that no one works as hard on their horses as our top boys.

The Seoul Olympics eventually came and went – medal-less as far as Britain's show jumpers were concerned, though David Broome came close to winning the individual bronze. The dust began to settle. Deprived of a place in Nations Cup teams, Milton had a few easy months before sweeping all before him at the Horse of the Year Show in October and subsequently at Stuttgart and Bordeaux. Then came Olympia. And a year in which the lows had very much equalled the highs as far as the Bradleys were concerned came to a shattering end. They wrote off their 'Milton Volvo' on the way home and very nearly wrote themselves out of the Milton story, too.

Owning Milton, then, has not been a trouble-free bed of roses. But the good days have far outnumbered the bad ones, and Doreen and Tom have the vast satisfaction of seeing Milton brilliantly fulfilling Caroline's expectations. They know, too, that in their choice of John Whitaker as Milton's rider they have helped establish the most successful show jumping partnership in the world. They rejoice in the pair's successes; they feel the occasional disappointment, though they, too, are the first to say that 'horses are not machines'; they admit that once or twice they have felt a little annoyed when John has missed a major jump-off because of a time fault. But, when all is said and done, they say quite categorically: 'No one would ride Milton better than John.'

CHAPTER 18

THE OLYMPICS

John went into 1992 with his sights firmly set on a record third World Cup, scheduled during Easter week in Del Mar, California. Things were to turn out very differently.

Refreshed from his winter break, Milton won two good classes in Antwerp at the end of February. However, not wanting him to peak too early, John did not start him in the World Cup Qualifier and rode Gammon instead. The following week in Dortmund, Milton had a warm-up outing in the Nordrhein-Westfalen Prize, in preparation for the World Cup class – where he jumped a double clear to finish fifth, beaten only by the clock.

The build-up to Del Mar seemed to be going to plan, until his arrival at the next show on the World Cup circuit, s'Hertogenbosch: Milton was found to have a minor fitness problem. 'He had some infection in his off-fore foot,' John explained:

> He had a bit of dirt in an old nail hole and it was too far up to dig it out so we poulticed it. He wasn't lame and we didn't think it was going to be too bad, which is why we didn't put him on antibiotics. But it didn't improve as quickly as we'd hoped so we had to give him a course of antibiotics after all and then of course he couldn't jump.

The horse missed both s'Hertogenbosch and Paris but was clearly going to be fit to jump in Zurich at the end of March. It was during his preparations for the valuable Swiss show that John received the news he had most wanted, but never expected, since he had been given the ride on Milton. After chatting about another matter, Doreen Bradley added, 'You can take him to Barcelona if you want to.' Milton, the horse the selectors had described as '50 per cent of any team' was on his way to Barcelona.

Most people in the sport had been sceptical about Milton's chances of going to the Games. Many had totally dismissed the possiblity. Doreen Bradley's words of four year's ago were evidently forgotten: 'If the Games had been closer to home it would be a different matter . . .' The Bradleys had discussed the subject with their daughter Judith and decided that Milton should be allowed to take his chance, assuming the selectors wanted him.

As for the World Cup, as so often happens with horses it was Milton himself who resolved the whole question. Returning to competition in Zurich, he jumped double clears in both the Grand Prix and the lucrative European Classic and finished third in the jump-off for each, adding another £13,500 to his earnings.

'He felt really good,' John recalled, 'and the plan was to give him a good rest

MILTON, WITH MASCOT, AT THE 1992 OLYMPIC GAMES. HAS HE JUST BEEN AT THE POLO MINTS OR IS HIS TONGUE OUT TO THE BARCELONA WEATHER?

before Del Mar.' However, the day before he was meant to go off to Frankfurt to join the plane taking the European horses to San Diego, John rode him and he did not feel 100 per cent.

There was heat in his near fore fetlock and although he was only slightly lame it hurt when you touched it. He must have twisted it though we don't know how or when. He could have done it in the stable or when he was turned out. He had been having a couple of hours in the field each day. He is not as daft these days when we turn him out as he used to be, but he still has a buck and he could have done it out there.

The disappointment of missing the final was alleviated by the prospect of taking Milton to Barcelona. Of course there was no question of the selectors not wanting him in the team, and the next few months were spent in getting and keeping him fit to do justice to the biggest challenge of his career. Since he had nothing to prove, he was not required to undertake the Olympic 'trials' and his competitive work was kept to a minimum. John's prime aim was to make sure that he stayed sound, while at the same time giving him enough jumping to keep him fit.

Milton attended the 50th-anniversary Royal Windsor Show in early May; he jumped in just one class and finished fifth. On the Saturday night he pleased the crowd by parading with that other grey equine legend – the former top steeplechaser Desert Orchid.

Next came the Hickstead Nations Cup meeting at the end of the month. John's primary target was the Grand Prix in which he had the benefit of a late draw. Milton, jumping fluently and executing several tight turns brilliantly, was well up on the clock going to the water ditches near the end of the course, and looked all over the winner, but he just brushed the back rail off the second last fence and finished third. Not wishing to overtax the horse at this stage, for the first time in seven years Ronnie Massarella did not put him in the Nations Cup team.

Milton returned to the Sussex show ground 10 days later for the Royal International's first running in its new home. John started Milton in the King George V Gold Cup, where they finished sixth, then followed the Henderson Grand Prix which was also designated an Olympic trial. Milton threw down a tremendous challenge with a fast clear in the jump-off, only his fellow Olympic short-listed rivals Tim Grubb and Denizen managed to do better to snatch the £10,000 first prize.

His one Nations Cup competition, *en route* to Barcelona, was in Dinard where he jumped a superb double clear, though the team was beaten by France. After that the British Olympic horses travelled by road to Spain, stopping off to compete in Royan on the way. Milton had three outings including two rounds in the Puissance. He jumped three clear rounds in the Grand Prix and finished fifth. He arrived in Barcelona exactly a week before the team championship looking fit and well.

The facilities at the Réal Polo Club were excellent, with spacious warm-up arenas and smart newly built stable blocks to which the riders added fans in an endeavour to alleviate the discomforts associated with temperatures in the nineties and 70 per cent humidity.

Ronnie Massarella deliberately asked John to start in the warm-up competition on the Saturday during the hottest part of the day to make sure that Milton could cope with the draining climatic conditions. He jumped the first six fences immaculately and John then pulled him out, satisfied that all was well. Milton demonstrated his *joie de vivre* a few minutes later as the rug thrown over his loins began to slip, and Milton's hindquarters suddenly shot up into the air to dislodge the offending garment. John sat limpet-like in the saddle, for a brief moment looking distinctly startled.

The course provided by Spain's Nicolas Alvarez de Bohorques for the marathon Nations Cup on August 4 was technical and generally met with the riders' approval. The one dubious fence was the last, an unusually wide Liverpool, comprising a set of planks over some 14 feet of water. As a fence it was perfectly jumpable, but its position with the morning sun behind it, and going away from the collecting ring at the end of a long track, was at best injudicious. John was not alone in thinking it an unfair question, and it was significant that exactly half of the first 46 horses were in trouble there. Once the sun had risen higher in the sky and the fence was out of shadow the rest of the field of 87 jumped it infinitely better. Had Nick Skelton's horse, Dollar Girl, not taken exception to it and been eliminated for three refusals in the first round, the team would have won the bronze medal. As it was they struggled from the outset and brilliantly though Milton went, he could not salvage the situation single handedly.

If anyone believed these Games had come too late for a horse approaching the autumn of his career, they had only to watch the way in which he powered his way faultlessly round the 14 fences to change their minds. John had brought him to the peak of fitness, had taken a bit of weight off him to help him cope better with the heat and he had never gone better. However, John did reveal afterwards that he had only just managed to clear the 15ft water jump in the first round. Positioned only seven strides after an oxer, it took a good deal of impulsion to clear it and John determined to ride the oxer differently in the second round.

 Alas his tactics did not work: he tried to get Milton to jump it more steadily, and to the right, in order to have more room to approach the water. Milton overjumped the oxer and that resulted in his rider still having too little room in which to increase the pace. There was a splash as Milton's off forefoot landed short of the tape and four faults went up on the scoreboard. It was to be his only mistake of the day. He finished the Olympic team championship in equal fourth place behind the three horses who had completed double clears. No one could have asked for more and it is only sad for him that his team-mates, with the exception of Mon Santa, did not go well enough to put Britain in the medals.

Milton was assured of his qualification for the individual final, on the last day of the Games, limited to the top 46 on points. In fact, John did not need to start him in the third qualifying competition on the Friday. Originally it had been assumed that this class would be compulsory for everyone, in order to ensure that, unlike in Seoul, all the horses would be required to jump the same number of rounds. In its wisdom the FEI had managed to word the newly formulated rules in such a way that the class became optional. This, coupled with the fact that the course provided by de Bohorques was too long and too big at this stage of the proceedings, led to a fiasco.

Many horses amassed cricket scores, some were retired by their disgruntled riders and the majority of the top horses did not even start. The paying public not surprisingly voiced its disapproval both during the competition and for a considerable time afterwards. Milton meanwhile was keeping cool and conserving his energies for the last day.

Whatever errors they committed on other days, there was obviously nothing the organisers could do to influence the weather on the morning of the final. A storm of Wagnerian proportions struck Barcelona, temporarily flooding both the streets and the polo club. The show jumps blew over like so many matchsticks: the arena looked like a beach with the tide coming in and there was no option but to delay the start. The competition finally began 40 minutes later, the rain came down in sheets and lightning and thunder raged all around.

No one can say for sure how these conditions affected the first dozen or so horses – they surely could not have enjoyed them – and as for the riders, trying to sit in a sopping wet saddle must have been about as easy as perching on a bar of soap. Most onlookers felt that a further delay would have evened the odds for everyone.

Hubert Bourdy, bronze medallist in Stockholm, retired in protest after faulting at the water and it was desperately sad to see Jos Lansink and Egano being eliminated for three refusals. By the time Milton came to jump conditions had improved considerably. Clear rounds had been achieved by Germany's Ludger Beerbaum on Classic Touch and by Dutchman Piet Raymakers with Ratina Z. John needed a clear

THE FENCE WHICH ENDED MILTON'S OLYMPIC CHALLENGE: HIS BELLY BRUSHES THE BACK RAIL OF THE BIG OXER GOING INTO THE DOUBLE. ALTHOUGH IT DID NOT FALL, MILTON TRIPPED ON LANDING AND WAS UNABLE TO JUMP THE NEXT FENCE

if he was to stay in touch, and Milton obliged in spectacular style. Once again a water jump of maximum proportions was included, this time at four coming out of a turn. The little fence on the take-off side had some white bollards in front of it which made the horses stand off, and John seemed to change his mind about Milton's stride as he came in. Milton seemed to arrive at it wrong, but he stretched out and cleared the tape as if nothing had happened.

Again coming to the big treble combination at 11, he looked a long way off the first element but Milton reached out to clear the back rails of the oxers. As he swept over the second part of the double at 14 to finish clear within the time, an individual medal looked his for the taking. Only one more horse went clear, the comparatively inexperienced Irish, ridden for the USA by the immensely skilful Norman Dello Joio. Four clears, three medals, it was all to play for.

The course for the second round, limited to the top 22 horses, was seriously big, with no fewer than eight wide oxers, including a double at four. Only one horse before Milton had less than two fences down, most had double figure scores. Milton was the first of the clear rounds to go and it was now up to John to put pressure on those who followed. He started well, easily clearing the first three fences. Then came the drama: Milton seemed a long way off the first part of the double and brushed the back rail with his belly during the steep descent. As he landed he tripped and was almost on his nose. John sat as quiet as a mouse as his partner struggled to regain his balance then gathered him together in an effort to jump out. Milton's head came up, he saw the next big oxer, sized it up in a split second and knew he could not jump it. Swerving out to the side the pair had to retrace their steps and all hope of a medal was gone.

As the clock went ticking on Milton cleared the double at the second attempt, and John swung him round to the big line of fences on the far side of the arena, desperately trying to claw back some time. The treble, a vertical followed by two oxers set on very long distances, had caused problems for the majority of the field. Milton obviously shaken by his slip, was now backing off the oxers: he reached for the first and hit the back rail, reached for the second and broke the back rail. Thoroughly unsettled, he took the front rail off the third last and finished the day with 19.25 faults in 14th place.

Looking at the overall performances in the Nations Cup and the individual final, and discounting that unsatisfactory third qualifier, only two horses jumped three clear rounds, the ultimate gold medallist Classic Touch and the runner-up Ratina Z. Four horses finished with two clears over two days, Moritz for Sweden, Egano, Genius and Milton. Disappointing, certainly, that there was no medal to crown his career. Yet two clear rounds and four faults over Olympic courses scarcely constitute failure. But for that unlucky stumble the end might have been very different.

But then, that's show jumping!

MILTON'S RECORD OF RESULTS

NATIONS CUPS

	Faults		
	Round 1	Round 2	Jump-off
1986			
Hickstead (GB 2nd)	12.75	5.50	
Rotterdam (GB 1st)	0.25	0.50	
Calgary (GB 2nd)	0	0	0
1987			
Hickstead (GB 5th)	4	0.25	
Aachen (GB 2nd)	0	0	4
Falsterbo (GB 2nd)	4.25	0	0
Dublin (GB 2nd)	0	NP	
Rotterdam (GB 4th)	0	0	
St Gallen (GB 1st)	0	0.50	
European Champs			
Calgary (GB 2nd)	0	NP	
Toronto (GB 2nd)	0	0	
1988			
Hickstead (GB 3rd)	0	0	
1989			
Hickstead (GB 3rd)	0	0	
Rotterdam (GB 1st)	4	4	
European Champs			
Calgary (GB 1st)	0	0	

1990			
Hickstead (GB 1st)	0	0	
Stockholm (GB 3rd)	4	0	
World Champs			
Calgary (GB 1st)	0	NP	
1991			
Hickstead (GB 2nd)	0	0	NP
St Gallen (GB 2nd)	0	4	
Aachen (GB 3rd)	0	0	
La Baule (GB 2nd)	4	4	
European Champs			
Calgary (GB 1st)	0	NP	
1992 (to end August)			
Dinard (GB 2nd)	0	0	
Barcelona (GB 7th)	0	4	
Olympic Games			

Total starts: 25
Total rounds jumped: 49
Clear rounds (including jump-offs): 33
Double clear rounds: 11
Winning teams: 7

OLYMPIC GAMES

	Individual placing	Team placing	Placings in the 2 competitions (penalties/faults in brackets)	
1992				
Barcelona	14	7	= 4 (0-4)	14 (0-19.25)

WORLD CHAMPIONSHIPS

	Individual placing	Team placing	Placings in the 3 competitions (penalties/faults in brackets)		
1990 Stockholm	2	3	9 (7)★	=6 (4-0)	2 (0.5-0.75)

★One fence down, 7 time penalties

WORLD CUPS

Finals

	Overall Placing	Placings in the 3 competitions (penalties/faults in brackets)		
1987 Paris	=5	16 (10)★	=7 (4)	1 (0-0)
1988 Gothenburg	8	26 (8)★★	2 (0-0-4)	=3 (0-4)
1989 Tampa	2	3 (0)	18 (4.5)	2 (0-0.25)
1990 Dortmund	1	1 (0)	2 (0-0-0)	2 (0-4)
1991 Gothenburg	1	3 (0)	=9 (4)	1 (0-0)

★ Two fences down, 5 time penalties each

★★ Two fences down, 4 time penalties each

Qualifiers

Total starts: 35

Placings in top five: 24 (7 wins, 6 second, 2 third, 4 fourth, 5 fifth)

Clear rounds (including jump-offs): 64

Volvo cars won: 9 (2 in Finals, 7 in qualifiers)

NB Milton also won the 1987 Qualifier in New York with a double clear round. European riders competing in North America have the choice of going for World Cup points or not. John Whitaker chose not to therefore in the official results the horse who finished second is credited with winning the event.

Qualifiers (officially designated Preliminary Competitions) may be one round with one jump-off against the clock or one round with two jump-offs, the second against the clock.

EUROPEAN CHAMPIONSHIPS

	Individual placing	Team placing	Placings in the 3 competitions (penalties/faults in brackets)		
1987 St Gallen	2	1	3 (0)	1 (0-0.50)	3 (0-5)
1989 Rotterdam	1	1	1 (0)	=6 (4-4)	1 (0-0.5)
1991 La Baule	5	2	1 (0)	=6 (4-4)	=7 (8-4)

MILTON'S JUMPING RECORD 1986–July 1992 (all placings for which he received prize-money)

Show	Class	Placing
1986		
Rufforth Park (Nat)		6
CSI-W Antwerp	Table A3	3
CSI-W Dortmund	**Table A3**	**1**
	WC Qualifier	4
CSI-W Paris Bercy	WC Qualifier	= 5
CSI-W s'Hertogenbosch	Table A3	=6
	Grand Prix	5
Royal Windsor (Nat)	Grades A & B	2
CSIO Hickstead	Table A3	4
South of England (Nat)	AIT	5
CSI Birmingham RIHS	Table A3	= 8
	Grand Prix	**1**
	Daily Mail Cup	3
CSIO Fontainebleau	Table A3	4
	Grand Prix	4
CSI Wolfsburg	Table A3	9
	Grand Prix	12
World Champs Aachen	Table A4	3
	Table A3	2
CSI Royan	Grand Prix	4
CSI La Baule	Table A3	3
	Grand Prix	3
CSI Dinard	**Derby**	**1**
CSIO Rotterdam	Grand Prix	7
CSI Stockholm	Table A3	2
	Table C	2
	Table A4	**1**
	Grand Prix	2
CSIO Calgary	Table A3	5
	Table A3	4
	Grand Prix	**1**
CSI Wembley HOYS	Table A3	7
	Leading SJ of Year	3
	Table A3	= 3
	Grand Prix	2
CSI-W Brussels	Table A4	9
	Table A3	**1**
CSI-W Bordeaux	WC Qualifier	8

Show	Class	Placing
CSI-W London Olympia	Table A3	4
	WC Qualifier	= 10
	Table A3	=7
	Grand Prix	2
1987		
Rufforth Park (Nat)	Grade A	6
CSI-W Antwerp	Table A3	= 8
	World Cup Qualifier	2
	Victor Ludorum	6
CSI-W Dortmund	Table A3	17
	Table A3	6
	WC Qualifier	2
CSI-W Gothenburg	**Grand Prix**	**1**
	WC Qualifier	2
World Cup Final Paris	First Leg	16
	Second Leg	= 7
	Third Leg	**1**
	Final Placing	= 5
Oldcotes Charity (Nat)	Grades A & B	4
	AIT	7
CSIO Hickstead	**Table A3**	**1**
CSI Birmingham RIHS	King George V Gold Cup	3
	Grand Prix	5
CSIO Aachen	Table A3	2
	Grand Prix	6
CSI Hickstead	Table A3	= 6
	Dubai Cup	9
CSIO Falsterbo	Table A3	3
	Derby	3
CSIO Dublin	**Table A3**	**1**
CSIO Rotterdam	**Table A3**	**1**
	Grand Prix	**1**
European Champs St Gallen	First Leg	3
	Second Leg	**1**
	Third Leg	3
	Final Placing	2
CSIO Calgary	Grand Prix	= 21

CSI Stuttgart	Table C	3
	Table A4	**1**
	Table A3	9
	Grand Prix	3
CSI Wembley HOYS	Table A3	7
	Leading SJ of Year	2
	Table A3	3
	Grand Prix	3
CSIO New York	Table A3	5
	Grand Prix	5
	WC Qualifier	**1**
CSIO Toronto	**Table A3**	**1**
	Table A3	**1**
	Grand Prix	2
CSI-W London Olympia	Table A3	2
	Table A3	**1**
	WC Qualifier	= 10
	Grand Prix	5

1988

Markfield Equestrian (Nat)		7
CSI-W Antwerp	Table A3	5
	Grand Prix	4
	WC Qualifier	= 7
CSI-W Paris Bercy	**Table A3**	**1**
	WC Qualifier	**1**
CSI-W Dortmund	**Table A3**	**1**
	Grand Prix	**1**
CSI-W 's-Hertogenbosch	**Table A3**	**1**
	WC Qualifier	**1**
World Cup Final	First Leg	26
Gothenburg	Second Leg	2
	Third Leg	= 3
	Final Placing	8
Oldcotes Charity (Nat)	**AIT**	**1**
CSIO Hickstead	Table A3	7
	Grand Prix	3
CSI Birmingham RIHS	**Daily Mail Cup**	**1**
	King George V	
	Gold Cup	2
	Grand Prix	**1**
CSI Franconville	Grand Prix	3

CSI Zurich	European	
	Classic	5
	Grand Prix	**1**
CSI Hickstead	A3	5
	Dubai Cup	= 5
CSI Mondorf Les Bains	Grand Prix	6
British Equestrian C.	Grades A & B	4
CSI Wembley HOYS	**Table A3**	**1**
	Table A3	**1**
	Masters	**1**
	Grand Prix	2
	Leading SJ of Year	1
	(on points)	
CSI Strasbourg	Grand Prix	3
CSI Stuttgart	Table C	2
	Masters	**1**
	Table A4	3
	Grand Prix	**1**
CSI-W Amsterdam	WC Qualifier	4
CSI-W Bordeaux	**Table A4**	**1**
	WC Qualifier	7
CSI-Brussels	Table A3	2
	Table A3	4
	WC Qualifier	**1**
CSI-W London Olympia	Table A3	5
	WC Qualifier	3
	Grand Prix	6

1989

CSI-W s'Hertogenbosch	Table A3	5
	WC Qualifier	5
CSI-W Paris Bercy	WC Qualifier	2
CSI-W Dortmund	Table A3	3
	Table A3	11
	Grand Prix	**1**
CSI-W Geneva	**WC Qualifier**	**1**
CSI-W Antwerp	Table A3	8
	Table A3	6
	WC Qualifier	5
World Cup Final Tampa	First Leg	3
	Second Leg	18
	Third Leg	2
	Final Placing	2

CSI Cannes	**Grand Prix**	1
CSIO Hickstead	Grand Prix	3
CSI Birmingham RIHS	Table A3	1
	King George V Gold Cup	2
CSI Franconville	Grand Prix	4
CSI Zurich	Table A3	10
	European Classic	1
CSI Hickstead	Table A3	2
	Table A3	= 5
European Champs Rotterdam	**First Leg**	1
	Second Leg	= 6
	Third Leg	= 1
	Final Placing	1
CSIO Calgary	Table A3	3
	Table A3	10
	Grand Prix	4
CSI Bremen	Table C	3
	Table A3	= 4
	Table A	= 1
	Grand Prix	2
CSI Wembley HOYS	Table A3	1
	Table A3	2
	Masters	1
	Grand Prix	5
CSI Stuttgart	Table C	3
	Masters	1
CSI Vienna	Table A3	1
	Grand Prix	3
CSI Maastricht	Table A3	2
CSI-W Bordeaux	Table A3	2
	WC Qualifier	= 7
CSI Frankfurt	**Grand Prix**	1
CSI-W London Olympia	WC Qualifier	3
	Grand Prix	2

1990

Arena UK	Grades A & B	4
CSI-W Antwerp	Table A	2
	Table A3	1
	WC Qualifier	= 11
CSI-Paris Bercy	**WC Qualifier**	1

CSI-W s'Hertogenbosch	**Table A3**	1
	WC Qualifier	1
CSI-W Gothenburg	Table A3	2
	Grand Prix	1
	WC Qualifier	= 5
World Cup Final Dortmund	**First Leg**	1
	Second Leg	2
	Third Leg	= 2
	Final Placing	1
Oldcotes Charity (Nat)	AIT	2
Royal Bath & West (Nat)	Grade A	2
CSIO Hickstead	Grand Prix	2
CSI Birmingham RIHS	Table A3	2
	King George V Gold Cup	1
	Grand Prix	2
CSI Franconville	**Table A3**	1
	Grand Prix	2
CSI Zurich	European Classic	5
CSIO Luxembourg	Grand Prix	3
World Equestrian Games Stockholm	First Leg	9
	Second Leg	= 6
	Third Leg	2
	Individual Final	2
CSI Mondorf les Bains	**Table A3**	1
	Grand Prix	10
CSIO Calgary	Table A3	7
	Table A4	10
	Grand Prix	14
CSI Wembley HOYS	Table A3	3
	Masters Qualifier	4
	Masters	1
	Grand Prix	2
CSI Stuttgart	Table A3	10
	Table C	1
	Grand Prix	6
CSI Vienna	Grand Prix	3
CSI Maastricht	Table A3	2

1991

South View Equestrian	**Grades A & B**	1

CSI-W s'Hertogenbosch	Puissance	= 10
	WC Qualifier	2
CSI-W Dortmund	**Table A3**	**1**
	Table A3	6
	WC Qualifier	4
CSI-W Paris Bercy	WC Qualifier	4
World Cup Final	First Leg	3
Gothenburg	Second Leg	= 9
	Third Leg	**1**
	Final Placing	**1**
Royal Bath & West (Nat)	Grade A	3
CSIO Hickstead	**Grand Prix**	**1**
CSIO St Gallen	Table A3	11
	Table C	5
CSIO Aachen	Grand Prix	3
Great Yorkshire (Nat)	Grade A	2
	Grade A	**1**
European Champs	**First Leg**	**1**
La Baule	Second Leg	= 6
	Third Leg	= 7
	Final Placing	5
CSI Mondorf les Bains	Table A3	4
	Grand Prix	7
CSIO Calgary	Table A3	5
	Grand Prix	3
CSIO San Marino	Table C	15
	Grand Prix	2
CSI Frankfurt	Table A4	12
	Accumulator	4
CSI Paris P de V	**Grand Prix**	**1**

CSI-W London Olympia	**Table A3**	**1**
	WC Qualifier	= 8
1992		
CSI-W Antwerp	**Table A3**	**1**
	Victor Ludorum	**1**
CSI-W Dortmund	Table A3	6
	WC Qualifier	5
CSI Zurich	Table A3	3
	Grand Prix	3
	European Classic	3
Royal Windsor	Grade A	5
CSIO Hickstead	Table A3	5
CSI Hickstead RIHS	King George V	
	Gold Cup	6
	Grand Prix	2
CSI Arnhem	**Table A3**	**1**
	Grand Prix	11
CSIO Dinard	Grand Prix	5
CSI Royan	Grand Prix	6
CSI Paris	Grand Prix	2

Key: Table A3 = international class, one jump-off
 against the clock
 Table A4 = international class, two jump-offs,
 the second against the clock
 Table C = speed class, faults penalised in seconds
 Grade A/B = class jumped under national rules
 AIT = Area International Trial
 WC = World Cup
 Nat = National Show

Milton's Prize Money

At end 1984	£1,126
Won in 1985	£15,186
1986	£71,617
1987	£91,742
1988	£147,820
1989	£216,029
1990	£182,737
1991	£193,985
(to mid Sept) 1992	£77,960
	£998,202

Although by mid September 1992, Milton's official career earnings totalled £998,202, during six and a half seasons with John he had either won for him, or at least contributed to, many bonus awards of cars. Awarded as rider prizes, the value of these does not appear on a horse's winnings record, nor do the monetary prizes given to members of Nations Cup teams. The exact worth to Milton of such awards has not been calculated, but there is no doubt that at some unrecorded time during 1991, he quietly became show jumping's first millionaire.